MAGGIE ROBIN

HERCULES
The Bear

For Mari ti,
Bearhugs and [...] es
from Andy. Maggi e Hercules

NOEL COLLINS PUBLISHING

StoonHan
1993

X

ACKNOWLEDGEMENTS

Copyright © Maggie Robin, 1981

First published 1981 by Noel Collins Ltd., 2 Dundonald Street, Edinburgh

Editors: Charles MacLean
Simon Scott

The publishers would like to thank the following organisations for providing pictures of Hercules without which this book would not have been possible:
The Daily Record, Daily Express, Daily Star, Daily Mirror, Sunday Mirror, Daily Mail, Sunday Mail, Sunday People, Glasgow Evening Times and Cinecosse Ltd.

ISBN 0 907686 04 4

Printed in Scotland
by William Blackwood & Sons Ltd, Edinburgh.
Phototypesetting by Adset Limited, Glasgow.

Contents

This book is dedicated with affection and gratitude to the
Islanders of Benbecula

Grizzly bear

1 GRIZZLY BEAR

Hercules is sleeping as I write this with his head on my feet. Earlier he was playing with the cushion that is now peeping out from under his enormous bottom, tossing it into the air and catching it in his paws. I told him that I didn't want him to burst it and he looked at me as if to say, "Come on, Mum; what do you take me for?", tucked it under his tummy and settled down to watch television.

It is a raw afternoon in November. The icy rain is coming down the glen in great swathes of grey and battering against the old house. Andy has gone out to chop wood for the fire. He cuts it in logs a yard long and we put them straight into the enormous hearth blazing beside me. On days like this, when the fire is stacked high, it is useful to have someone like Hercules around to help me lift them.

This room, our sitting room, is probably very like your sitting room — with armchairs and sofa; T.V. and photos on the walls — an ordinary sized room with ordinary objects. The house it is in, our home, is the Sheriffmuir Inn, off a narrow backroad that leads to the A9, the main road to the North of Scotland.

The Parish of Sheriffmuir — there isn't really a village — is between Stirling and Dunblane.

When I look out of the window here on a fine day there is no sign of humankind. The Ochil Mountains rise around us — a vanguard of the great mountains that form the centre of Scotland. We are on the edge of the old Highland Line, and the people round here would have spoken Gaelic in the old days. Further down the glen the land is cultivated in small fields and there are plantations of pine trees. In front of the Inn, and on the other side of the road there is a fast flowing burn, fed from the mountains, in which Andy and Hercules love to play in the warm weather.

The house is over three hundred years old. It was here where the famous Battle of Sheriffmuir was fought on a misty November day in 1715, and, indeed was used as the headquarters of the Earl of Mar, who

Home Sweet Home

lead the Jacobite army. Mar and his highlanders were trying to break
through to join the Jacobites who had risen in the North-west of Eng-
land, when they met the Duke of Argyll at the head of a disciplined
army of Hanoverian troops. They fought all day in the mist and the
Clan Macrae were slaughtered to a man. In the end there was no con-
clusive victor. Sometimes, on dark days like this, one can almost imagine the kilted clansman moving down the hillsides with gory broad-
swords in their hands . . . If stones could speak our old Inn would have
some strange tales to tell, but perhaps none stranger than the story I
love to tell about the battle of wits between a man and a grizzly bear.

Yesterday someone came to the Inn to see Hercules. He had spent
many years in the North of Canada and in the Arctic and had seen bears
in the wild — both grizzly and their near cousins the polar bear.

He refused to come into Hercules' den and stood at the door in-
credulously repeating "I don't believe it; this can't be real; I must be
dreaming", while Herc kissed and cuddled his Master.

Two years ago, when he was working in the north of Canada, he
had joined the search party for a friend who had gone off alone on a
fishing expedition. They found his tent and there were bears' footprints in the snow all round.

He prayed that his friend had been knocked senseless by the first
blow from the huge hungry creature that had found the camp, and
refused to go to the actual spot where his friend had finished his days.
All they found there were some shreds of clothing, a belt buckle and his
false teeth . . .

On another occasion, further north, he had watched a polar bear
sitting over a hole in the ice, patiently waiting for a seal to pop up.
After a while a large seal weighing about 200lbs, duly appeared and
slithered into the frozen air. With one movement the bear was on him,

7

and with another he had delivered a massive swipe with his front paw that lifted the broken seal into the air and flung it like a toy over the ice. When the bear had moved off he crept down and measured just how far the seal had been flung by that one blow: it was 66 feet!

I could well believe it. When Hercules was younger there was a tree trunk in his den. It was about four feet high and about two feet in diameter. Oak; and so heavy that even Andy couldn't lift it and had to rock it from side to side to move it about the den. Hercules would pat it from paw to paw sliding it easily across the floor, like a child with a toy. Once when he was in a particularly mischievous mood he picked up the log and used it as a battering ram to knock down a wall!

In Yellowstone Park, in the U.S.A., a grizzly once killed a large black bear with a single swipe. The punch was so strong that it knocked the black bear against a tree 16 feet away!

Hercules stirs in his sleep and stretches out a front paw like a pile driver. As with all bears in captivity, the claws on his front feet were drawn when he was a baby. If they are not drawn, they break off in middle age and never stop bleeding. Otherwise he is as he would be in the wild — unmuzzled, uncollared, still with a full set of teeth. His canine teeth are 2 inches long.

My old Chambers Encyclopaedia solemnly says of the great cuddly heap at my feet that "No animal in the New World is more formidable". Red Indians believed that he was created to be more powerful and more clever than all other creatures: once he was created, runs the legend, even the god that made him, Manitou, had to flee to the top of a mountain to escape him. He would have had to flee fast, what is more, for over a distance of up to 150 yards a grizzly bear can run as fast as a good horse!

In spite of their fearful reputation — "more fierce and carniverous than any other bear except the polar bear", says the encyclopaedia — and in spite of the numerous exaggerated stories of the Old West in which bands of grizzly's attack homesteads during hard winters, bears are in fact timid creatures.

One experienced bear hunter of 100 years ago remarked in his memoirs "I have pursued a great many bears, and every one of them fled before me; not a single one showed any intention of defending itself." Only when they are surprised are they likely to attack; particularly when there are cubs or if they are disturbed when hibernating, and this they do by rearing on their hind legs, swinging their front

Polar Grizzly

At home in the Rockies

Water Bears

paws and growling. Most experts agree that this posture is basically a display, meant only to intimidate the foe, and certainly a bear usually knocks it's opponent down with a swipe and then moves away.

If they are attacked, of course, bears will attempt to defend themselves, and there are numerous stories — again from the Old West — of bear hunters being chased. In 1805 a Mr. Meriwether Lewis was chased for 100 yards by a badly wounded bear and two days later his companions emptied eight rifle shots into a bear and still could not stop it coming at them!

Still today in parts of Canada and the United States where there are still bears, they are held in awe and respect, and not a little fear. I spoke to someone recently who had asked an Old Timer backwoodsman what he should do if he met a bear. The old fellow sucked on his pipe and said with deliberation that the first thing to do was to climb a tree, then it depended on whether the bear was a black bear or a grizzly. "How will I be able to tell" said my friend. The old timer replied "Wal, if it's one of them there black beyers he'll jist come up th' tree after you; but if it's a Grizzly, why, he'll jist knock that ole tree down . . ."!

People walking in the National Parks where bears are to be found wear 'bear bells' round there necks to warn of their approach and avoid the possibility of surprising any bears. But accidents occur; funnily enough, bears who live close to humans, and rely on scraps and garbage left behind by picnickers for the main part of their diet, become even more dangerous, and there are always stories of picnickers being eaten up by a bear, even though it happens very rarely.

Andy and I are always conscious of the risk attached even to the great big softie snoring in front of the fire beside me, but we know him very, very well now, and he us, and it would take a brainstorm or something to make him run amok.

Mind you, every now and then I hear stories that give me pause for thought. Last year Smokey, a black bear, used for wrestling, killed his owner's wife. The bear was chained and muzzled, as all wrestling bears apart from Hercules are, and the wrestler's wife had never had any contact with the bear and was never allowed to touch him. She was blonde, like me, and the same age. And she was called Maggie!

Usually after an 'accident' like this the bear is shot — though, in this case the Canadian Government took the bear into care! Andy and I left a document with our lawyers stating that should anything happen to us, no matter what, Hercules is not to be harmed . . .

Herc is growling in his sleep. He is probably dreaming about his terrible ordeal in the wild when he was lost in the Outer Hebrides. I will tell you all about this in its place. First I must tell you how a man won the love and trust of a grizzly bear, something that the whole world said was impossible, and in order to do that I must introduce you to my husband, 'Grizzly' Andy Robin.

'Come on Mum;
stop writing and read me a story'

Grizzly Andy Robin

—— 2 GRIZZLY ANDY ROBIN ——

Little did I know as I was getting my horses ready to go to the Perth Agricultural Show on that hot August morning in 1972, that the day would prove to be one of the great turning points in my life. As I busied myself in the stables making sure that my horses were groomed and that the horse box was prepared, I had no thoughts about the day other than that I hoped to do well in the events for which I was entered and that I might meet a few friends there.

As a farmer's daughter I was well used to going to Agricultural Shows, which were always full of ruddy faced farmers dressed in their best tweed suits with their endless talk of barley and wheat, top soil and seed potatoes. For some people they aren't the most exciting places in the world, but I always longed for them as they gave me an opportunity to ride in competition.

I had never been to the Perth Show before as I had preferred, until then, to compete in the more local show which took place on the same day. A simple twist of fate made me decide to go to Perth that day, and how glad I was in the coming years that fate made me do so.

I arrived at the show a short while before my first event was due to begin and having tacked up the horses and collected my numbers from the show Secretary, I had plenty of time to wander around the stalls.

As I strolled from the newly mown ring back to my horse box I was suddenly aware that I was being stared at. Turning round to get a better look, I found myself facing a large suntanned man with the most piercing blue eyes I had ever seen. He was not so much tall, as big, and to my consternation he was smiling at me, although I know that I had never set eyes on him before. I began to blush and dropped my head quickly to avoid his stare which seemed to be saying "You don't know me, but you will".

I hurriedly made for my horse box and began busying myself with the final preparations. As I struggled with saddles and bridles, I put the brief episode out of my mind and by the time I had changed into my breeches and navy jacket I had forgotten him.

However, as I was warming up in the collecting area outside the show ring I noticed the suntanned gentleman was once again standing behind me, and trying to ignore him I went about the business of limbering up each horse, taking them in turn over the red and white fence that stood in the middle of the practice area. I could not help glancing in his direction and each time I did so I was met by the same penetrating stare and wry smile, and each time I felt myself turning crimson with embarrassment.

Luck was not with me that day and although I managed one clear round I finished the event with a miserable fifth place. Feeling suitably humbled, I made my way back to the horsebox to wipe down the horses and put on their travelling bandages.

I was stabling that night with Mr. and Mrs. Drummond who were directors of the show and as they were not yet ready to leave, I had time to kill. As I sat and watched the other competitors leading horses back to horse boxes I saw the crowd beginning to gather round a smaller ring that had been hastily erected in the centre of the arena. I decided to investigate, and made my way into the thick of the crowd.

Ladies champion show-jumper

I managed to find a place for myself at the front of what was clearly a wrestling, or boxing ring, just as two burly figures stepped into it. At that moment I noticed that the man who had stared at me earlier was standing just in front of me, only now he was wearing a pair of blue trunks and had a tartan towel slung casually over his huge muscular shoulders. It was now obvious that he was at the show to wrestle, and seemed to be a popular figure judging by the number of backslapping farmers who surrounded him.

I fidgeted self-consciously trying to appear nonchalant as he moved towards me. As the bout started he drew me into a one- sided conversation, explaining holds and throws, pins and falls, such information being deftly interwoven with a smooth chat-up routine.

He was on next and I was slightly shocked to see someone who had been talking to me in a relaxed way suddenly change into a grunting heaving brute as he mercilessly pummelled his opponent, and yet I had to admire the ease and efficiency of every superbly executed movement, which quickly led to the submission of his foe.

After the bout I left the showground wondering at the roughness of my new acquaintance who had been led triumphantly from the ring while his opponent had been carried off on a stretcher. I wondered if our paths would cross again and doubted they would, which was probably a good thing as I knew he was not the sort of man my mother would want me to bring home for tea!

How wrong could I be. The very next day the persistent stranger rang my home, though it is anyone's guess how he got my number, and after much persuasion I reluctantly agreed to go out with him that night.

As the weeks passed, we began to see more and more of each other, and for the first time in my life I found myself becoming deeply interested in something other than my horses. Andy could not have been further removed from the boy next door, but as we got to know each other we discovered that we both had a deep love of animals and the outdoor life. At first my parents, while not openly saying so, made it clear that they did not approve of my association with Andy. Like all parents they wanted the best for their children and expected me to settle down and marry a kind, honest farming man like my father. They had heard stories from their friends that Andy was a ladies man with a chequered past, a disreputable job, and an insecure future.

In time when they realised that trying to dissuade me from seeing him was useless and they came to know him better from his frequent visits to our house, they began to grow fond of him in despite their pre-conceived ideas.

Gradually Andy began to win my parents respect with his infectious enthusiasm and his determination to get on in life. Andy had to be determined, because he began life in Stirling, the son of a hard working miner, in a community where there was no real alternative but the pit and sons followed fathers in going down the mine. It was a life of unremitting toil and considerable hardship, and seeing his father's life and what prospects lay before him Andy swore at an early age that he would do everything in his power to avoid going down the mine, and vowed to work in the open air.

Grizzly Andy, aged 5

As a child Andy loved being outdoors and developed a love for animals that kept him constantly in trouble. His parents had to watch every penny carefully and they could not afford to keep a pet, nor was there room for one in their tiny house.

This did not deter Andy, who would befriend any animal he met and bring it back into the house. Time and again the family's evening meal would be interrupted by an indignant neighbour banging on the door asking if Andy had 'borrowed' their dog, and sure enough the animal would be found hidden in Andy's bedroom. It was not just the usual domestic pets that caught Andy's fancy. He would also smuggle in owls and rabbits that he found when roaming in the countryside.

When Andy was twelve he found a stray spaniel. For once he tried to find out who the owner of the dog was, but none could be found, and so he kept the dog, which he called Sammy, hidden in a shed and fed it on titbits taken secretly from the larder. Sammy was a natural retriever and would bring back anything that Andy threw for him, picking the object up in his soft mouth and laying it at Andy's feet. One day Andy took Sammy for a walk in the countryside near his home, and on the way they took a shortcut through a nearby farmyard. In the farmyard were a number of ducks, and Andy had considerable trouble stopping the over eager spaniel from picking up the ducklings that were waddling around the yard.

The next day when Andy came back from school he discovered two ducklings in the shed and no Sammy. He hurriedly put the ducklings into a sack and went off to deliver them back to the farm. When he got back home again he found Sammy in the shed with another duckling, and this time when he went back to the farm he ran into the furious farmer who was convinced that Andy had been stealing. Poor Andy was in trouble again!

Andy's first job was on a farm and his mother personally delivered him to the farmer in the hope that some hard outdoor work would begin to channel his energies in the right direction. But this was not to be, for he felt terribly hemmed in by the routine work on the farm, and one night he sneaked out of his bothy and ran away.

It was soon after leaving the farm that Andy at last found something he really liked doing when he was given the opportunity to start in the timber business. The work was entirely outdoors and was intensely physical and Andy thrived on it. In time, by working all the hours God gave him, he managed to save enough money to go into business on his own.

Going into business on his own meant just what it says and equipped only with a saw and a horse and cart, Andy would single-handedly fell the timber, load it, transport it and unload it. His capacity for hard work quickly earned him the nickname of 'The Beast' in the timber trade, for he became immensely strong.

One day after Andy had cut down a tree he noticed that a jack-daws nest was lodged in the fallen branches. There were two fledglings in the nest who had obviously been abandoned by their mother when the tree was felled. Andy's big soft heart couldn't let him leave the two helpless birds and so 'The Beast' adopted them. He called the two birds

The Beast

Jackie and Mary and raised them in his house. When the birds were fully fledged he released them but they would always come to be fed, and it was not uncommon for Andy to be seen with a jackdaw perched on each shoulder, and when Andy was working they would sit on the head of his alsation Rex. Sadly, one day as Andy was coming out of his timber store the birds flew to meet him and not knowing they were behind the door Andy opened it and crushed Jackie. Mary was heart-broken and within a short time she pined to death.

Not content with running himself into the ground at work every-day, Andy became involved in amateur boxing, but when he saw the damage the sport inflicted and after being reprimanded by referees for grappling in the ring, he turned his attentions to wrestling.

Discovering that he had a natural flair for the sport Andy took up wrestling seriously and started his career by attending the numerous Highland game meetings, that took place each summer all over Scotland. At one of the meetings Andy met a fellow wrestler called Willie Bell and they decided to go into partnership. The pair soon established themselves on the circuit and were among the most successful competitors in Scotland.

Andy and Rex   'Timber . . .'

'We'll be alright for firewood this winter'

'. . . but it'll be a job cutting it into kindling . . .'

Success followed success for the persistent Scot and when only twenty he won the World Cumberland Wrestling Championship. Having won the championship he was asked to go to Canada to take part in a festival of sport called "The Wonderful World of Sport", and join a select group of Scottish Athletes who were going to demonstrate Scottish Sports such as tossing the caber and throwing the hammer.

He set off for Canada in a second hand kilt with a breadknife stuck down his sock in place of a Skean Dhu! The show played to full houses throughout Canada and America and Andy grew more and more confident in his own abilities as a wrestler, and more professional in his handling of audiences.

Champion at the Highland Games

Partnership with Willie Bell

However, fate had decided that Andy was not to complete the tour. When the show got to Toronto it was discovered that there had been a mistake in the bookings at the Maple Leaf Gardens and instead of performing on the Thursday as they thought, the show was not to take place until the following night. The Thursday evening booking was a professional wrestling spectacular, and Andy with lots of free time on his hands, hung around the stadium while the auditorium staff prepared the ring. As he was about to leave he was approached by the promoter Frank Tunney, who said that one of the wrestlers booked to

On the receiving end

The unique and unbeatable Robin's Power Lock

appear that night had been injured in a fight on the previous evening and as they were desperately in need of a replacement would Andy have a go?

Eager for the extra cash it would provide he accepted and made his way back to the digs to get his kit together.

It was with some trepidation he entered the floodlit ring that night for his first major professional bout. But his nervousness was calmed as he heard the crowd, many of whom were Scottish Canadians, roaring their support when they saw he was wearing the kilt.

Andy won the bout and when he returned to his dressing room he was met again by Frank Tunney who offered him a two year contract to wrestle all over Canada and America. Always ready for adventure, Andy quickly signed the contract and over those two years he refined and polished his wrestling skills. His professional career was by now fully established and just when he should have been consolidating his position he agreed to take on the most hazardous bout of his life. He was booked to fight the Terrible Ted.

Terrible Ted was no normal wrestler. He was a black bear. At the time of agreeing to fight, Andy was not aware of this, but when told he agreed nevertheless; the bear would be chained and muzzled, and if Andy could hold his own he was guaranteed a thousand dollars in prize money.

The arena was packed that night, and the air heavy with anticipation. As Andy walked down the aisle and waved to the cheering crowd he became increasingly aware of just what he was letting himself in for. If Ted were to get a good grip he could easily crush the life out of him and it wouldn't matter one bit whether the bear was muzzled or not.

Ted stood in the middle of the ring, towering above Andy, making strange growling noises through his shiny black muzzle, and Andy swears to this day that if he hadn't been wearing the kilt and hadn't felt that he would be letting Scotland down if he didn't go through with it, he would have turned and ran.

Suddenly a thousand dollars seemed a paltry sum to be paid for risking one's life, and as he dodged the massive swipes of Ted's front paws, and manoeuvred himself out of corners where he might be trapped within the huge bear's grasp, Andy not only felt genuinely more threatened than he had ever been before, but he also recognised the enormous spirit of the magnificent creature.

TERRIBLE TED

In the following days he kept reliving the fight with Terrible Ted which had been so unlike fighting another man and yet strangely similar. In those few minutes an uncanny understanding had grown up between the bear and himself. An understanding that was only hampered by the fact that Ted was kept consantly chained and muzzled. "What sort of relationship could develop" thought Andy "between a man and a bear if that bear was treated, without fear, as a genuine equal?" From that moment onwards Andy determined that he would one day find out.

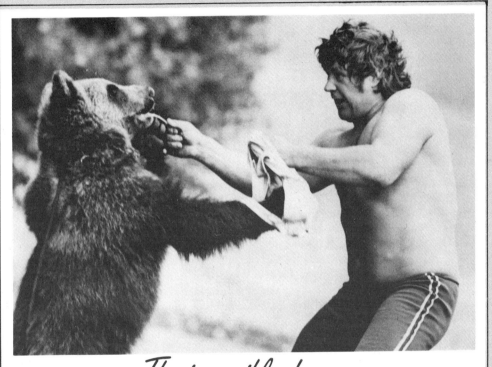

The impossible dream

— 3 THE IMPOSSIBLE DREAM —

Long before we were married, Andy and I agreed that we would do everything we could to share our lives with a wrestling bear. This was to be no ordinary wrestling bear, however, chained and trained only to entertain, degraded into a dangerous clown. That was not the idea. Andy had a vision of an animal that would spar with him on equal terms, a friend and companion whose dignity and independence would be recognised, and who would show the world that trust and companionship were the only ways to achieve results. A wrestling bear who would discredit for ever the tradition of bear baiting and wrestling with mutilated animals.

We knew that the chances were slender, and the responsibility enormous. A bear can live for 40 years and cost a fortune to feed. Our whole lives would have to be devoted to him.

Bears were so much a part of Andy that it never occurred to me to question his obsession. I met my first bear in the bear park on Loch Lomondside where we were enquiring about cubs. An enormous she-bear with two little teddy bear cubs crossed the road in front of our car. She came round and glared menacingly through the car window, which was mercifully closed, and then went on her way. I was very afraid, but nevertheless from that moment I was infected by Andy's enthusiasm.

Finding a bear to own was a different thing altogether. Zoos adopted an incredulous and snooty attitude towards us: they agreed it was preposterous to suppose that such unpredictable and extremely dangerous animals could be made 'pets' of, and they were not prepared to sell a bear into the barbaric slavery of chained performance. We thought at the time "What difference is there between chained performance and close imprisonment?" and tried elsewhere.

Then in December 1975 we heard that a she-bear in the Highland Wildlife Park at Kincraig was pregnant. We contacted Eddie Orbble, the director, and after meeting him said he was prepared to sell us a cub for £50, but he insisted that the cub remain with his mother until it was weaned: he didn't expect us to keep the cub for more than a week. At this time Mary, the she-bear, had not yet given birth.

There were three cubs in the litter, christened by Andy; Atlas, Hercules and Samson. Atlas was the largest, and Samson the smallest. They seemed more adventurous than Hercules, rolling about and playing with one another while Hercules stayed close to his mother. We saw them first in February, 1976, and were captivated by their antics, especially by little Hercules. He was already standing unsteadily on his hind legs like a little furry man and had a ring of white baby fur round his stumpy neck.

We left him to suckle under the expert and gentle care of Eddie and said that we would be back as often as we could to keep up with his changes. Over the next seven months we travelled to Kincraig many times, watching him grow in leaps and bounds, until the great day came when he would be ours.

We had borrowed a crate from Edinburgh Zoo and travelled up in the caravanette towing the horse box so as to be able to spend the night and leave in plenty of time for moving Hercules the next morning. That evening we drank mugs of cocoa and went over our plans with Eddie and his wife. Although we couldn't persuade them of the possibility of achieving what we wanted, at least he could see that we would take great care of his precious baby, and this in some measure allayed his doubts about letting us have Hercules in the first place. We were up with the birds next morning, impatient to get on with the difficult task of moving Hercules away from his mum and into the horse-box. He was 10 months old and weighed 13 stone: even at this age he was stronger than the average man. It was necessary to tranquilise him before moving him. Eddie gave him the shot while we all kept clear of his sharp teeth.

Even as he went under his little lip curled in a half-hearted snarl of defiance, but by the time he came round we were ready to go. Farewells were said and everyone agreed that they expected to see Hercules back within the month, but all were very interested to hear what the outcome of our adventure would be. We backed the trailer carefully down the cinder track and were off on the open highway to Sheriffmuir, stopping after an hour or so to make sure our precious cargo was safe, and have a bite of breakfast in a Little Chef restaurant.

Over the blue formica table we wondered nervously how long

Samson and Hercules

Proud father

26

Hercules would take to adapt himself. Would the movement of the horsebox throw him into a rage? Andy had saved a piece of roll and spread it with tomato ketchup as a treat for our new baby. He took it gently and his little sleepy eyes lit up as he licked off the sweet sauce.

We had built a spacious den for Hercules behind the Inn, very close to the back door. It was made of white emulsioned stone and connected to an area almost as big as the house itself which was securely surrounded by a high fence of iron bars. In the den were a couple of rubber tyres, a tree trunk and various other toys for our new baby, and beside it was a hayshed.

Our first task was to move Hercules from his crate into his new home, and this time it would be without any tranquilizer, so you can imagine the tingling nervousness we felt as we realised that anything could happen. Gently, we backed the trailer up to the small door of the den leaving just enough room to drop the ramp, and slid the heavy crate into the entrance. By this time Hercules was slowly and deliberately weighing the situation up as he stood up on all fours, fully awake and ready for action.

As we opened the sliding door of the crate he took off at a rate of knots, panic stricken, but thinking clearly enough to try and establish the best way out — and hopefully away from — these strange new people that now had such a say in his life. Within seconds he disappeared into his sleeping quarters, noticed immediately a gap between the top of the wall and the hayshed and frantically tried to climb up to it. He seemed to spot every potential escape route within seconds, his eyes darting this way and that and missing nothing. His instinct for survival had put him on the defence right away.

After about fifteen minutes he began to settle down and wandered from one part of his den to the other, sniffing at corners and handles. We watched him silently and then out of the blue Andy announced that if they were to begin getting to know each other there was no time like the present to start. We were still the enemy, but what would young Hercules' reaction be if a hand of friendship was offered?

It didn't take long to find out. Armed with a large carton of strawberry ice cream Andy entered the outside run. The cuddly little bear wore an expression of deep suspicion as he stood his ground, eyes wide with fear. Both parties then remained perfectly still, leaving it to the other to make the first move. After some time the little black button of a snout sniffed the air in the direction of the offered goodies and slowly took the first step towards the source of the smell. I was rooted to the spot as I watched Hercules draw closer towards Andy's outstretched hand. Then he was there; out popped his little pink tongue and he hungrily got stuck into the proffered peace offering.

It all seemed too easy — and sure enough, once the tit-bit was finished, the sharp white teeth — now bigger than the last time — were again sunk into Andy's hand of friendship.

Andy's free hand delivered a sharp smack on Hercules' snout and he quickly dropped his second 'snack', now very bloody, with a look of amazement. It was to be the first of many battles with the wild young creature.

As autumn turned to winter we came to understand the tenacious instinct for survival in our growing friend. Each day was spent planning and working around Hercules, trying to overcome every setback as we came upon it. After the bout with Terrible Ted in Canada, Andy had sought out the bear's trainer, Gene Dougouis and had learned a lot about the likes and dislikes of bears. Also he had been continually told of their innate treachery as a species.

His physical strength and agility, and his wrestling background, made him better able to dodge the swift snaps and buffets aimed at him by the young bear and very gradually his courage and kindness seemed to get through to the suspicious young creature and win a glimmer of respect.

It was two months before I could even touch him, and even then I had to withdraw from him very quickly before I had my hand mauled. It was a time of slow progress and many disappointments.

One of the earliest problems was to persuade Hercules to wear a collar and lead. It was like breaking in a stallion with very sharp teeth. Andy would move in as close as he could and catch him with a lasso : Hercules would tense his neck and dash about the den knocking Andy from wall to wall and diving in as often as possible to bite any part that he could reach. It was only superhuman determination that prevented Andy from giving up at this stage, but he knew that the moment Hercules felt he had the upper hand all that he had achieved so far would be lost.

No sooner was this hurdle crossed than we had to embark on the even more difficult task of persuading Hercules to wear a muzzle. He wouldn't have to wear it all the time — only when he was wrestling — but it was important to get him used to it as early as possible, and he

Bath-time

was now nine months old. All those who had trained bears said this had to be done before they were nine weeks old!

The first thing was, to have a muzzle made that fitted him properly. There were no ready manuals or text books to offer us guidance in this : it was a case of trial and error. The first muzzle was made of leather and consisted of a strap round Hercules' neck joined to two other straps around his nose that hung fairly loose. This was to get him used to the idea of having a 'bridle' on. To put it on him was a matter of bribery in the form of icecream, grapes and yogurt, and very quick reflexes when he decided he'd rather have a bite at our arms instead.

We continued this for about a month, and only after this time would he allow us to work about his head, slipping the muzzle on and off without fuss.

In December it began to snow. Hercules had been with us now for four months, and when we looked out of the window that morning after the first snowfall we saw him happily burrowing his way under the deep snowdrifts in his den. I made breakfast of porridge and cream for Andy and I, and a great pot of beans, eggs, cod liver oil and bread for Hercules. We topped this off with a large pot of tea with milk and sugar for all of us, and we were all ready for the day. Hercules rushed out of his den and followed us into the paddock on the long lead, rushing about madly diving into snow drifts until all you could see was his little furry bottom sticking up in the air against the brilliant white of the snow.

One of his favourite pastimes in the snow to this day is sledging. He learned the skill accidentally on a large plastic container that he found in the paddock, discovering that if he placed his big front paws on it he could then push at the ground with his back paws and slide easily down the hill!

By the early spring we really thought we had a chance of proving the experts wrong. Not only was Hercules still with us, but we seemed to be making daily progress in our relationship with him. It's true that he was by no means a household pet — it was not our intention to turn him into one — but neither was he the fierce creature that he had been when he arrived, and that most bears in captivity remained.

From the beginning of the 'experiment' the press had taken an interest, and they kept an eye open for developments as the months went by, tending to dwell on setbacks rather than achievements. There

Wild bear

Narrow escape

was, sadly, never any shortage of people to criticise and complain of danger. They usually took the line that 'it was for our own benefit'; that 'we didn't know what we were doing'; that 'we had no training in the handling of dangerous animals'; that 'sooner or later there would be a fatal accident'. In spite of it all we persevered; they could do little to harm us — or so we thought.

It was neccessary for us to obtain two licences to keep Hercules : a Performing Animals Licence, which would enable us to train him and to entertain others with him, and a new licence — introduced in April 1977 — the Dangerous Wild Animals Licence, which would enable us to keep an animal specified under the Act that introduced it.

The first licence could only be obtained if the keeper had some experience of working with the animal in question and could show that his treatment of the animal, and the conditions under which the beast was kept fulfilled the legal requirements. Local police and vets who had carefully monitored us since before Hercules' arrival lent their support to the application and the licence was obtained without any difficulty.

The second was a different matter. Being a new piece of legis-lation, the local Council was unsure of how stringent it should be, and since we were the guinea pigs they wanted to make absolutely sure.

Although we had not seen a copy of the Act, we were told that it applied to us and asked to send off details of the size of Hercules' den, the strength of the material it was built out of, the number of warning notices about the place and so on. We were well above the required standards and supposed that it would simply be a matter of time before the necessary piece of paper arrived.

We were wrong. The Stirling Council met once every fortnight and at meeting after meeting the application came up and was referred for further information. We couldn't believe it. Andy wrote to them suggesting that the surest way of judging was to visit the Sheriffmuir Inn and see for themselves, but they declined, preferring to continue 'considering' and 'referring' from the Council Chamber.

By this time it was becoming ridiculous and beginning to attract the attention of the local papers. It seemed that, although the Council could not find any legal grounds for refusing the licence, there were several councillors who did not like the idea of a grizzly bear roaming about the hills of Sheriffmuir and were determined not to be rushed in-to any decision. After several months even the councillors were look-ing for a way out and decided to visit the Inn.

'Seconds away . . .'   *First fall*

We were given pre-emptory notice of this and then were plagued at all hours of the day by the comings and goings of councillors, arriving without appointment and expecting to be shown round and given the full treatment.

We both felt irritated that these bureaucrats could arrive and roam about our home pulling at bars, opening doors and measuring things that had all been tested and measured before. Matters came to a head one Sunday with the arrival of a woman councillor.

I had been working hard in the bar all week and was enjoying a peaceful afternoon mucking out the horses. I was about to go for a ride across the moors when I noticed a heavily made-up elderly woman in an imitation fur coat making across the yard and boldly opening the gate.

'Down boy'

'May I have the first dance?'

"Can I help you?", I asked.

"I'm from the council" she said without stopping "I've come to see your bear."

I closed the gate she had left open and followed her to Hercules' den.

"There he is", I said "that's my baby".

She looked at me as if I was mad and, hauling the plan of the enclosure from her bag, proceeded without more ado to pace round the den poking and pulling at things. As I watched her I could not fail to be struck by the contrast between the natural grace of the wild creature behind the bars and the phoney elegance of the human outside. A comparison between their coats made me smile involuntarily — the one so rich and glossy, the other so dull and tawdry. At that moment Andy arrived on the scene. I grimaced at him to let him know that something was up.

Making up

House Trained

"Can I help you?", he asked.

"I'm from the Council: I'm here to see your bear", she said again.

"What do you think of him? He's a beautiful boy, isn't he?" asked Andy.

"No comment", was all she said.

"I beg your pardon . . ." began Andy but she cut him short, "I'm not here to explain to you what I mean".

I slid away to avoid the explosion. Andy has never cow-towed to anyone in his life, just as he has never bullied anyone. Small-mindedness and mean-spiritedness are alien to him, and where Hercules was concerned he reacted like a father would.

From the kitchen I saw the Councillor wither under Andy's broadside and the next she was in the bar, dragging away an astonished little man from his half-pint.

"I'll not have you drinking in this place," she said as she hurried him into her car and drove off, scattering stones.

Growing trust

———— 4 GROWING TRUST ————

It seemed miraculous to the doubters that within five months of Hercules coming to live with us we were confident enough in him to be able to accept an invitation to present him in public.

The invitation came from the promoters of the film 'Grizzly' which was to be premiered at the Odeon Cinema in Edinburgh in January, 1977. The film was about a ferocious killer bear in the Rocky Mountains that attacked and ravished unsuspecting campers and they wanted Hercules to perform the opening ceremony and take part in the press reception afterwards: he was sure to be a big pull.

The roads were clear of snow and we took Hercules down in the horsebox on the morning of the engagement. He seemed to catch our excitement and was eager for this new adventure, remaining unperturbed by even the strange noises of his first visit to the city. We didn't know where the cinema was and asked the way from a couple of pedestrians; once we had found it we were met by a police escort. Understandably nobody was taking any chances.

They directed us into a car park near the venue and stood about apprehensively while we checked that the cinema was suitable for Hercules. What they would have done if Hercules had run amok I didn't ask: they later told me that they did not for a moment expect that they would be prepared to allow Hercules to mingle with the public.

We returned to the car park and dropped the ramp. Two inquisitive brown eyes sparkled in the gloom. Andy went into the box, clipped on the lead and, giving the thumbs up led Hercules out into the car park.

Surrounded by policemen we walked up a brick lined corridor and entered the theatre by a door right underneath the huge screen. The audience no doubt expected a bloodthirsty monster like the bear in the film: they saw a large bear cub shyly blinking at the spotlights, and then intelligently he gained his confidence, Andy winked at me and I uncrossed my fingers. All would be well.

It went better than 'well'. It was a resounding success. Hercules behaved like a young filmstar and gambolled happily up the aisle looking for stray sweeties and smiling at the delighted audience.

We lead Hercules into the foyer at the front of the house where there was already a small crowd of interested onlookers. Hercules played up to them and made a bee-line for a large cardboard cut-out of the fierce hero of the movie. He considered it carefully and explored behind it and then to the delight of the onlookers proceeded to flatten it and pull it to pieces. It was all done in such a playful way that it seemed as if our young friend was clearly saying "I'm the star of this show: what do you think you're doing here?"

Onlookers and police roared with laughter. I went over to one of our policemen who had escorted us and asked his verdict: "He's been a perfect gentleman", came the reply, "Indeed, I've seen many a worse behaved dog. I think we can quite safely go home now".

I turned and looked proudly at my two boys capering in front of their admirers . . .

We were greatly relieved that the event had gone off so well and as we drove away from the Odeon we felt very proud of our baby, now napping in the horse-box behind us with a belly full of ice-cream and shandy. We stopped on the outskirts of Edinburgh to buy an evening paper, and to our surprise saw Hercules' broad face looking out at us from the front page. The press had pronounced the show a triumph!

As we drove further north the snow began to fall heavily again and by the time we reached the small road to our home it was clear that we were not going to be able to make it, towing the horse box. We pulled into Sandy Anderson's farm road and unhitched the trailer. "What about Hercules," I asked Andy. "We'll take him in the car with us", he replied. "It'll be better than walking on a night like this, and we have only three miles to go."

"Do you think that is wise . . ."

It wasn't. As soon as he was in the van Hercules lunged towards the front seats. I leaped out to safety while Andy tried to comfort the startled bear. There was nothing for it but to walk, and as soon as he was in the open air Hercules happily entered into the spirit of the thing. I drove the van on ahead and put the kettle on. As they came to the road end I watched with apprehension as Andy leant down and loosed the leash. I need not have worried: I gave a shout, Hercules pricked up his ears and bounded right into his den. We all three drank mugs of tea and

Winter walks

congratulated each other on a most successful day.

The snow fell for three days that week and the three of us were snowbound. It was a time of marvellous companionship and growing awareness of the powerful bond that was forming between us. We were able to let Hercules wander about without his lead as the snow was so deep that it made even him timid: he liked to feel in control of situations and he became concerned if he suddenly disappeared in a snow drift or had to bulldoze his way too far from the security of his warm den.

Winter turned into spring. My horses were back out in the paddock, frisky as they sensed the sap rising. They had been previously aware of Hercules from the start and we had made sure that they were kept well apart. 'Horses and bears don't mix', said the books, 'Horses have a deep rooted, primeval fear of bears'. In time, however, we decided to put these theories to the test.

At first the horses took to their heels whenever he came into sight. After each burst of speed they'd stop and turn to face the furry shape which always seemed to be able to corner them, even in the 20 acre field. They stared towards it and their nostrils flared until the shape grew too close for comfort, and once more they'd be off. Hercules couldn't understand this behaviour. He seemed to be puzzled by the fact that these creatures just didn't seem to want his friendship and preferred to retreat leaving him to wonder why his efforts to become friends weren't working. But daily cavortings paid off in the end.

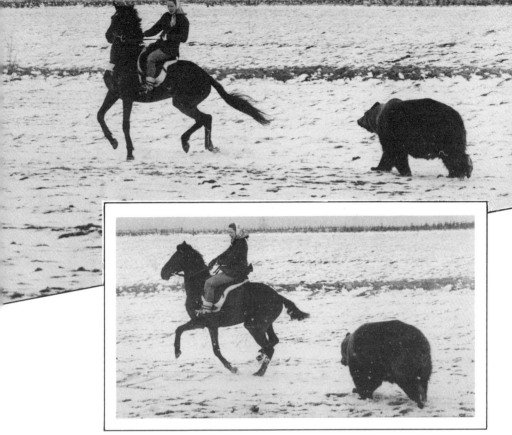

Catch me if you can

Sheriffmuir, a superb jumper full of guts and more intelligence than I have ever known in any other horse, became particularly aware of this persistent fellow who shared his field for an hour or so each day and began to develop a special bond with him. It happened gradually. They weighed each other up and seemed to think out each step carefully as they approached the imagined barrier that had separated them so far. Sheriffmuir knew he had speed as his trump card, just in case.

Hercules on his side seemed to acknowledge that the spindly bay didn't fear him and slowed down his movements when the little horse with the intelligent eyes came near: he seemed to sense that this was one he could get through to — a friend for the future, perhaps. We watched the two of them daily coming closer together, stealthily moving, until at last one sunny day they came nose to nose.

Sheriffmuir's tense neck lowered to greet the outstretched black button nose that Hercules offered. A quick sniff: a little snort and Sheriffmuir backed away a step or two, waiting, gingerly to see the reaction of the strange animal. Hercules seemed to sense that this was his chance to let the horse see that he meant no harm. He stood motionless: trying in his own way to communicate confidence to the other noble head that watched him cautiously from a few feet away. Andy and I stood rooted to the spot, trying to keep our excitement under control. "What a beautiful sight", I thought with pride welling up inside me as we waited for the next move.

Hercules' tactics were working. Sheriffmuir sensed that the outstretched nose was an offer of friendship and slowly stepped forward for another reassuring sniff.

Hercules sniffed back and then out came that long pink and black tongue to give the soft muzzle a great big lick to seal the bond. At last Hercules had made his point and won the confidence of the shy horses.

From that day Hercules' understanding of the timorous nature of his gentle friends grew. He often accompanied me as I schooled them and occasionally tried his skill over the small jumps I erected for him: he invariably ended up by mashing them into firewood!

Hercules is very possessive of Andy and I, and although he has become used to the horses he is put out if he thinks that we are paying too much attention to them and he'll show his displeasure by crying loudly and thumping his heavy metal pot on the ground until the noise becomes too much to bear and we give in and go and play with him for a spell.

We were aware of this when Allan, a friend who helped in the hotel, arrived with an accidental litter of kittens, that he could not possibly keep in his small house in Dunblane. He asked if we could keep them and try to find permanent homes for them if we couldn't they would have to be drowned.

They moved in, but by late afternoon one of the litter a little white bundle of fluff, looked unhappy and we brought her indoors. Hercules was perplexed by what was going on and sat sniffing at the wall which separated his den from the hay shed. When we brought the tiny white creature into the kitchen he started acting up diving about his den and peering excitedly through the kitchen window to spot its exact whereabouts. We settled the little kitten in front of the fire and hoped that Hercules would settle down too, but when the strange white creature didn't reappear from his kitchen Hercules sat dejectedly for a moment and then started to cry, his cry sounded just as if he was saying Mom over and over again.

Nip!

Ouch!

"You'll have to take the wee thing out Maggie," said Andy, "Hercules' jealous, he thinks his Mum and Dad have found someone else and he feels left out!" I picked up the kitten and carried him back to the others. Hercules seemed more than satisfied: he stopped his crying and swaggered round his den, once more he had made his point.

Then one morning as I was washing up the breakfast dishes I saw the mischievous little kitten disappear through the entrance to Hercules' inner den. I knew Hercules was inside on his bed of sawdust and rushed out to try and divert the little creature from certain disaster.

I slid back the side door to the main den and reached the inner door of iron bars in time to see Hercules raise a massive paw and bring it down on top of the tiny unconcerned creature. I was about to cry out but then checked myself as I realised that he had halted his paw within fractions of an inch of the kitten's back and was feeling it very gently. He often did this to things — for example he liked to gently run his paw round the contours of our faces — but I never expected that he would have such control over his immense strength that he could avoid crushing a kitten.

The kitten rolled over on its back and pressed its little feet against the huge foot above it, enjoying the game, and thereafter it would fearlessly sneak into the den in search of fun.

Another animal that crept into Herc's inner sanctum was Charlie the Pheasant. Charlie was a wild pheasant from the woods nearby who had discovered that there were often tasty scraps to be had in the den. We saw him so often, stalking proudly about the enclosure, that we could recognise him and even christened him.

Herc didn't seem to mind him when he cheekily strolled into the inner den and pecked up food from right under his nose. Then one day Andy called to me to the outer run and drew my attention to a mass of pheasant feathers. "Looks like Hercules' finally had enough of cheeky Charlie." Strangely, we could find no sign of Charlie's body and since Herc always refused to eat raw meat we doubted whether he had gobbled him up. It was a mystery.

And then, about three days later, who should emerge from the den but a very shamefaced looking Charlie — with hardly a feather on his body!

One would have thought that the terrified bird would have learned his lesson from such an experience, but not a bit of it. He returned even more regularly than before. We put grain out for him and he has become quite tame. His feathers have now grown back again and we see him almost every day.

We have often thought what it could be that Charlie found to eat in the den, before we started putting out grain, that is. He must have been attracted by the hay in the barn for there was not much in Hercs' diet that would be good for pheasants, and anyway he left very little of what he was given to eat.

For breakfast we gave him between one and three dozen eggs (it depends on the time of year: he gets more in summer, and on who feeds him: Andy spoils him!); six tins of spaghetti hoops in tomato sauce and a loaf of bread. This is all washed down with a gallon of sweet, milky tea — and it must be milky, mind, or he will knock over the pail and demand more!

For lunch he has fruit — usually grapes and apples — and for dinner he has a main meal of cooked meat, with vegetables such as carrots, cabbage, or broccoli. The meat is often ox hearts cooked in tomato, lentil or oxtail soup, or, as a special treat, roast chicken, which is his favourite dish.

In summer he requires about 15lbs of meat a meal! We top off the daily dinner with a whole bottle of advocat which he loves and which is very good for his coat! He also likes curries and spaghetti bolognese, but surprisingly enough he is not terribly keen on honey.

His meals are served on a silver tray which came by courtesy of Trust House Hotels. We were staying in one of these establishments and borrowed the tray to break Herc's breakfast eggs into. He enjoyed eating off it so much that when Andy asked him to give it up, he wouldn't. Andy explained all this to the chef who was angrily asking for his tray back. "I'm afraid you will have to get it from him yourself" Andy said "Herc won't give it to me." The chef left his kitchen and came out to the truck. I don't think he had really believed it when he had been told that we wanted the tray to feed a bear: when he was confronted by a nearly full grown grizzly, weighing over 40 stones he nearly fainted! Andy introduced them and Hercules was very friendly but adamant about his tray. The chef kindly gave it to him as a present.

When Hercules was not much more than a year old we decided that we must buy him his own truck: sharing a trailer with horses was not good enough, and anyway he would soon be too big for the horsebox. We thought that it would be more pleasant for him if he were able to see what was going on, and after long consultations with our local blacksmith, Bob Burnett, Andy decided to buy a Toyota pick-up truck onto the back of which Bob could fit a cage.

When it was done it looked very smart indeed: it remained to be seen whether Hercules would like it. He approached cautiously and sniffed the suspicious new thing and it took some time to coax him into the cage itself. We left him to sit in the sun for an hour or so, and acclimatise himself to his new travelling den, and then Andy drove gently down the road. At first Hercules jumped about and rocked the truck

'I do like my food'

Enough of this walking; let's go for a swim?'

frantically, but then he settled down and took up a position standing on his hind legs behind the driver in order to watch where they were going. From then on he always took up this position in the Toyota.

As we travelled about further afield with Hercules, it became necessary to get an even bigger 'travelling den' for him. We decided the best thing would be to secure a second hand single decker bus and convert it into accommodation for both ourselves and Hercules.

It didn't look much, that first day we saw it, neglected and scruffy looking with its panels painted a drab blue and inside showing signs of much wear and tear. But its engine had a steady beat and we drove it home full of plans for renovation. A complete face-lift was called for and we set about working on it through the cold days and long nights of the winter.

'What 'ave we got 'ere then?'

'Quite comfortable really . . .'

47

Herc didn't like it at all. We tried to persuade him to have a look inside and told him it would be his new travelling den, but he would have none of it and wouldn't come within twenty feet of the bus. It was clearly going to be a struggle to persuade him into it.

First the seats had to come out to make way for the den in the back compartment and a living area in front for us. Then the exterior of the coach buffed down to the bare metal to give a base for the new colours it was to be painted in. Bright red on a cream base with lots of stars and fancy lettering. The inside was plush and comfortable and the last job of all was the fitting of a bright new wire mesh cage from the black-smiths.

It looked sensational when Andy drove it into the yard: now to see what Herc thought . . .

The cage at the back seemed to give him confidence, or maybe he just liked the bright colours, for he walked bodly up to his new caravan and after sniffing around it for a few moments, stood up on the stair leading into our living room and peered at it from the safety of the bottom step. Then he jumped in and investigated. Having done this he was more than happy to check out his cage and sat in it with a proprietorial air.

Since Hercules has become a super-star we have bought yet another bus to transport him about the place. This one was made especially for him and us, and has every conveivable mod-con.

Having a travelling home for the three of us became necessary from early on. When Hercules was only a year and a half old Andy had to go away for a couple of days. The whole time he was away Herc did nothing but lie morosely in his den mopping and wondering where his pal had gone. I did my best to cheer him up with some of his favourite snacks, but after he had greedily swallowed them he lapsed back into his black mood.

The first thing Andy did on his return was to visit his chum, but Herc would have none of it. He felt that he hadn't been consulted and that accordingly he had every right to be moody. It took a lot of sweet talking on Andy's part to coax him out of his huff!

On another occasion we both decided that we deserved a short holiday. Our friend Allan agreed to look after the Inn and take care of Herc for the three days that we planned to be away and we towed a small speedboat up to Loch Etive with the intention of exploring the coast.

'Phew . . . at last'

It's alright for you: I'm still wearing my winter coat

The hotel had a beautiful location, the staff were very kind and our room was comfortable. After unpacking we went down to the Loch to launch the boat and then returned to our room to shower before dinner.

Although the food was good, and typically highland our meal was a sombre affair and our conversation non existent. Without admitting it to each other we felt like a couple of traitors who had abandoned someone who needed us. We knew that Allan would take great care of Hercules, but we remembered Hercules' moodiness when Andy was away and couldn't bear to think of him sitting morosely in his den, wondering where we were.

By the end of the meal we were utterly miserable and in the very opposite to a holiday mood. I telephoned Allan, with Andy standing beside me listening to what he said: it was clear that Hercules was as miserable as us: there was no point in staying any longer, for what value a holiday if you spend it wishing you were elsewhere.

We left first thing next day and, as soon as we arrived back, went straight to see Hercules. His black mood this time was twice as bad as his huff on the last occasion, and we had to spend at least half an hour bribing him with sweeties in the sitting room before he regained his usual cheerful mood.

After this we decided that whenever we went on holiday in future we would have to take Hercules with us: he is as much a member of the family as any vulnerable child would be.

And a very jealous child at that. We know that Hercules feels that we belong to him as much as he belongs to us. He is prepared to share us with others occasionally, just as we are prepared to share him, but only on the strict understanding that it is temporary and that we will quickly revert to our close family role. I am often asked whether I plan to have children and Andy and I have talked about this at length. The conclusion we have reached, and the answer I give, is that Hercules would regard another member of the family as a betrayal of the very special, and singular relationship that we have built up.

After all, what is a successful family but a close group of individuals who love and depend upon one another? Children grow up and leave the nest and find loved ones and people to depend on elsewhere. Hercules has only us and we are proud to shoulder the responsibility of his love, for God willing, the next forty years.

'Left on my own,
I take to drink . . .'

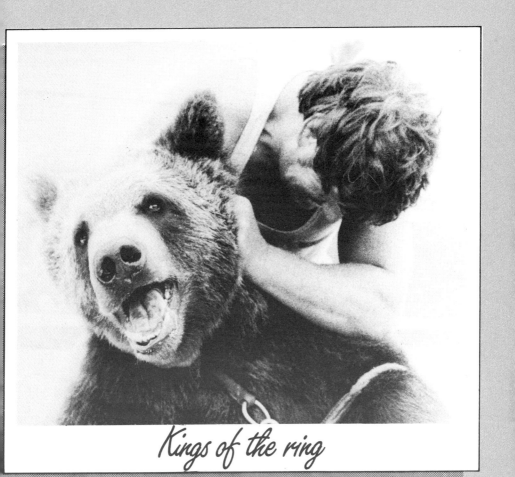

Kings of the ring

— 5 KINGS OF THE RING —

Andy's first encounter with a bear had been in the ring and from the start his hope was to share his love of wrestling with our adopted son. Hercules needed no encouragement — after all — the sport originated from North American Indians watching the antics of bears in the wild — the difficulty would be to prevent him being carried away with enthusiasm so that he would use his full strength, and either accidentally or in a fit of pique snap Andy's back or give him a swipe that would brain him.

Hercs sheer bulk and strength meant that Andy had to use all his strength and the skill gained from years in the ring to keep up with him and gradually teach him about human limitations. Beginning with casual rough and tumbles, he was gradually able to employ more complicated wrestling moves and to teach Hercules what fun it could be to slip out of a hold and put his human opponent on the defensive. Everything depended on building up Hercules' trust and making him realise that the very last thing in the world Andy wanted to do was to harm him. It required great patience and delicacy, for Hercules was acutely suspicious of every new move.

One day they were wrestling in the snow — by this time Herc was fairly addicted to the sport — Andy was tempted to put the 'scissors' round his sparring partner's neck, a move he had not tried before. In doing this he accidentally clonked Hercules on the top of the head. Hercules immediately sprang free and ran to me for protection and comfort, pressing into the back of my legs and using me as a shield to ward off the formidable Andy! It was one of the most tender moments I think I have ever experienced. He was just like a confused and frightened child, running to his mum for protection. Andy spoke softly to him, kept reassuring him and repeating "I'm sorry, baby, I'm sorry", while Hercules peered nervously over his shoulder. After a while they made up, Hercs' faith was restored and they resumed their game.

It was some time, and only after a lot of careful training, before Andy was again allowed to put the 'scissors' on, and by that time Hercules was so accomplished a wrestler that he didn't take long to break the hold!

As Hercs confidence and trust in us grew he took great pleasure in showing off his prowess as a wrestler before an audience. Every Saturday, once our guests at the Inn had finished their supper, we invited them to move up to the top part of the lounge so that we could clear the lower part in readiness for a most unusual cabaret.

Once all was ready in would trot Andy and Hercules — the latter delighted and excited by the chatter and laughter from his admirers. The noise soon quietened, however, once the pair started their act. Rolling about the floor, grunting and groaning in fine style, the audience were spell-bound as first one then the other champion managed to take the upper hand. It was quite clear though, who they supported, and as Herc warmed to the sport and pinned his opponent to the mat, waiting for the count to three, spontaneous applause and laughter rang to the rafters.

It was hot work tumbling about with a half-grown bear in front of a roaring log fire and after a short while the round would end and drinks would be served to the contestants, To the delight and amusement of our guests Herc would comfortably sit back on his haunches and quickly drown a pint of his favourite tipple, lemonade shandy, held expertly between his massive front paws. A proper gent!

One particularly strenuous night Hercules was eager for more than his customary pint. Another was fetched for him and still his thirst was not quenched. After a couple more he was satisfied and ready to return to his den. He appeared to be unaffected by his over-indulgence — except for a mischievous grin and a certain bleariness about his eyes — but when we reached the cold fresh air at the kitchen door his legs simply buckled under him and down he went! He, of course, was very contented with the situation, lying on his back on the kitchen floor waving his legs happily in the air. Our problem was to shift about 30 stones of bear back to his bed. It took ages, but stumble by stumble we made it and one boozy bear was safely tucked up to sleep the sleep of the just! The next morning he looked distinctly hung over . . .!

As Herc grew bigger it became impossible to continue with these Saturday evening demonstrations in the small lounge, but by this time the pair were training for Hercules' first professional contest, which was to be held in Perth in August, 1977.

The summer weather was perfect for the long runs and exercise bouts that filled the month before the great day. Astonished drivers on the Sheriffmuir road would see man and beast embracing by the roadside, Herc with his massive arms wrapped round Andy's muscular shoulders, or perhaps gently tracing the contours of Andy's face with his huge paw as they rested after a strenuous work out. Cars would pull up, small traffic jams would form. Groups of unbelieving motorists would approach to within what they considered to be a safe distance and fire questions at the pair. Andy would enthusiastically reply on behalf of both of them and Herc would grin good naturedly.

As the month of intensive training went by Herc became more and more adept at the game. Now each time Andy tried a new manoeuvre, his companion seemed to consider it carefully, and invariably by the time Andy tried it again he had thought of a counter move. Indeed, such was Hercules' intelligence that he began to invent his own holds and to employ them with great gusto — to the considerable discomfort of his sparring partner.

Although the relationship that had developed between the two was so close and affectionate, Andy was by no means blind to the dangers of wrestling with a grizzly bear. As Hercules developed his muscles and became heavier, so Andy had to trim his weight down and build his strength up so that, in the event of something untoward happening, he could jump clear. Even the backs of strong men were

Working out

like matchsticks to the powerful bear.

As well as the physical preparation of the contestants we had to devise some way of preventing Herc from rolling between the ropes and out of the ring during the fight. We had noticed that whenever he felt unsure of things — strange noises or traffic, for example — he liked to retreat into his den or into the pick-up truck that we transported him in and stay there until the danger had passed. (This in itself gives the lie to the popular belief that bears are ferocious aggressors and will attack without thinking, rather they know that survival depends upon not risking the unknown, avoiding if they possibly can, attacking only if cornered and desperate.)

In the end we decided to construct a low, lightweight wire fence which could be erected in sections round the ring. This turned out to be a great success for, while leaving the crowds view uninterupted, It seemed to give Hercules a feeling of security, and security was particularly necessary on this occasion as the contest was to be held indoors, in the Perth Icerink, and Herc was used to fighting in the open air.

We set off early, Andy driving the pick-up with Hercules and I following in the Volkswagen, towing the horsebox for Hercules to rest in privacy. When he arrived, Hercules would have none of it and after posing for photographers for half an hour, stubbornly refused to nap in the horsebox. He wasn't going to miss anything, and, after all, he was the star of the show and every whim must be pandered to! So he stood in the pick-up in the slow drizzle, watching everything that was going on with keen interest, as the audience arrived and an expectant murmur rose from within the rink.

It was to be a five bout spectacular. The first act warmed the audience up, and the second was between two attractive girls who quickly showed the spectators that they were more than just pretty faces and gave an excellent account of themselves. By the interval the audience were in a good mood and the air of expectancy for what was to come had reached fever pitch. We brought Hercules from the truck to his dressing room under the grandstand and he nervously looked about him and up at the ceiling, which was reverberating with the excited stamping of the spectators. I had made some tea and hoped that this, and some of the grapes that he loved so much, would reassure him that there was nothing to be afraid of. The moment of truth would come five minutes later when we had to encourage the young fellow to allow us to muzzle him.

He hated this, and would only allow Andy to do it when he was calm and confident. This evening he was shy and jumpy and with every glance at the ceiling my hopes that he would allow us to put the thing on dwindled. My heart was pounding, my throat was dry and my hands were shaking. While I comforted him and fed him grapes, Andy slipped his collar on. All I could think about was the hundreds of people out there who had come especially to see my two men do their stuff. How awful it would be if we let them down. I was oblivious to everything in the room except for the muzzle in my crazily shaking hands; petting him and comforting; Andy soothing him — "It's alright, old son; its going to be fun; you have friends out there."

Herc stared about, unconcerned, and then quite suddenly lowered his big wet nose and allowed Andy to strap on the hated muzzle. All would be well. Herc had come up trumps again. I squeezed my mans hand and hugged my big baby, the latter looked at me as if to say "What's all the fuss about. I'm a professional. You don't think I'd let you down, do you?"

56

I went out into the stadium and heard the master of ceremonies announcing that there would be a five minute break before the main event to allow for the fence to be erected.

"The event you are about to watch," I heard his voice echoing tinnily through the stadium, "is unique in the history of wrestling. Not only will Andy Robin attempt to go 15 minutes with a grizzly bear and thus create a new world record . . . The previous record is a mere 5 minutes . . . but he will do this without the bear being attached to a restraining rope. No one has ever risked this before. The danger is so great and the strength of these creatures so immense that there has always been a handler in the ring with the animal, and the animal has always been restrained by a rope and choker so that it can be dragged off when things go wrong. . .

"in spite of this tragedies abound: you may recall the tragic occasion when Jimmy Chipperfield, one of the most respected bear experts of modern times, attempted to wrestle with Bruno the Bear, back in 1935, in the London Paladium. Mr Chipperfield lost a lung after only 4 minutes . . ."

I needed no reminding as the adrenolin coursed through my veins. I prayed silently that Hercules would not forget himself in the excitement and would control his will to win.

"I must ask you to remain absolutely silent, ladies and gentlemen, until Hercules had entered the ring . . . Are we ready?" He turned to the men putting up the fence. "Ladies and Gentlemen: it is my pleasure to introduce to you Grizzly Andy Robin, and Hercules the Bear . . ."

There was an awed silence. I hurried back to the dressing room to tell the boys the curtain was up. They were deep in consultation, Andy with his arm round Hercs' shoulders; Hercules with his chin on Andy's knees.

As we walked towards the ring, our hollow sounding footsteps were the only sound to be heard. Herc walked beside Andy with his body pressed tightly against his master's legs for re-assurance, his brown eyes darting this way and that, taking in his surroundings, watching the pale faces of the spectators craning to catch a glimpse of him.

When he saw the familiar ring he walked eagerly towards it and jumped like an old pro straight through the ropes and onto the ring, where he turned to his partner as if to say "come on then, what are you waiting for?" I shut the gate in the fence and took my seat.

'One small shove and I'll have you out of the ring'

'Ah, that's good'

Andy picked up the mike to say a few introductory words, but Hercules would have none of it. He bounded across the ring, reared up on his hind legs and tackled Andy from behind, almost causing him to swallow the mike. The fight was on.

Hercules' talent that night was a joy to watch. With intuitive intelligence and elegant skill he escaped from all the holds that Andy put him into. Then he would take the lead and pin Andy to the canvas. The crowd roared their applause. But with his agility and experience Andy would manage to break free from his 30 stone opponent, only to be knocked to the floor once more.

Hercules was enjoying every minute and would look up now and then to make sure he was receiving the attention he deserved from the spectators. Then he turned back to the fight and proudly head butted Andy across the ring, to the delight of the audience. Once Andy had recovered from this set back he resumed the offensive and tried to throw Hercules over his leg, but his opponent was too wily, and dexterously shifted his feet back and forth without even glancing down, seeming to know by intuition which leg Andy was aiming for and lifted it out of reach before Andy could get at it.

"Ten minutes" rang out through the p.a. system.

The sweat ran off Andy in little silver rivulets under the spotlights and even Hercules was beginning to pant a little. Neither was in the mood to give up, though, and Hercules was as determined to win as Andy was to avoid being crushed. Only a minute to go. I could slacken my grip on the pint shandy I was clutching as I realised that everything had gone perfectly according to plan and the danger was almost past. The bell rang it was over. The bout was pronounced a draw and the world record was well broken.

As one, the crowd rose and gave my boys a standing ovation. Months of work and worry now seemed worthwhile. Andy undid Hercules' leather muzzle and handed him the well deserved pint. Hercules had already spotted it and sat down on the canvas in anticipation — it was gone in moments!

By now the crowd had surged round the ring, shouting congratulations and asking questions. One of the first there was Eddie Oddie from the Wildlife Park at Kincraig. "Well done Andy," he said "Hercules is in beautiful condition. I never thought you'd manage it. I thought I'd have him back in the park within a week."

The press were also there, looking, I thought somewhat disappointed. I was later told by a friendly journalist that they had come to see Andy killed. . .

The Perth Icerink event had highlighted the problem of having to have Hercules muzzled during wrestling bouts. At first we thought it was only a temporary thing that he would get used to his muzzle again before too long, but as time went on it was clear that he was not going to change his attitude towards it.

On such occasions as he allowed us to put it on him, as in Perth — usually now by breaking a couple of eggs into it by way of a bribe — he looked at us as if to say "our relationship is based on trust, and yet you do not fully trust me." We dared not. When wrestling in the wild, bears use their teeth to haul each other about, catching hold of each others tough, loose, pelts and using the hold thus gained as a levering point. Hercules could not be expected to realise that human skin is no protection against 2 inch long teeth and Andy would have been, at least, terribly scarred. Indeed in the thrill of a bout Hercules could so easily become carried away, that even worse might happen. But in the months following the Perth event he became more and more reluctant to having the thing put on him, until he devised a way of beating us at our own game.

The way was very simple: he would not wrestle. He would sit on his haunches in the corner looking imperiously about him, sulking openly. No begging or bribing would persuade him to shift. It reached the stage when we could not rely on him to even play up to his audience.

He would just act as if he didn't know what was going on and he would often search me out from the crowd with his eyes and look to me for support in the stand he was making.

One day his resistance to the muzzle became active rather than passive and Andy narrowly escaped a very hard beating. It was during a bout in Dumfries in the spring of 1978, about 8 months after the Perth event. Andy and Herc were billed to wrestle and they had attracted a large crowd to the Loreburn Hall. We had managed to persuade Hercules to put on his muzzle by breaking an egg into it, but he was particularly listless and it had taken an unusually long time to get it on. Both of us were apprehensive in case he played up; and sure enough, once he was in the ring he wandered about morosely and would not be enticed into wrestling.

Andy had explained to the audience that, unlike many other

'I jolly well won't fight in a muzzle'

animals, Hercules was not simply conditioned to perform. If he didn't want to fight, he wouldn't and that's all there was to it. The audience would get their money back.

He tried all Hercules' favourite moves, offering him grapes and pleading with him but Hercules was surly and unhelpful, wanting all the time to come over to me outside the ring. Then quite suddenly he seemed to think "to hell with this, I'll show him I mean business" and, rearing up on his hind legs tried to clout Andy so hard that it would have smashed his skull. Andy dodged and realised immediately from the look in Hercs' eye that this was for real. He wasn't trying to do Andy serious injury, but he was determined to make his point, and when bears do that they are certain to do serious injury. The next seven or eight minutes were very tense as Andy tried to dodge and calm Hercules down. At last he succeeded and he turned to the audience to apologise that there would be no wrestling that day and to offer them their money back. The audience, however, were delighted with the show. They had not realised that Hercules had been seriously trying to injure his partner and that Andy had been seriously tying to keep out of his way, and felt they had had their money's worth.

It brought to a head, though, Andy's and my concern about muzzling our friend.

Hercules was far more to us than a way of making money. He was far more to us than a pet. He was far more to us than proof of a successful zoological experiment in animal/human relationships. He was a friend, a beloved companion — a son.

We loved him more than anything else in the world. Our lives were intertwined even more than the lives of many members of a family. We could not bear to see him unhappy.

Andy loved wrestling, and so did Hercules for that matter, and without the muzzle this pleasure, and considerable financial benefits that it brought, would have to be sacrificed. Our relationship was based on complete trust, the muzzle was a breach of that trust, and Hercules might understandably be suspicious of other things if this breach was not filled.

It did not surprise me when Andy came into the kitchen one morning, took down the muzzle and put it away. Our boy meant too much to us to be exploited in this way.

Hercules seemed to realise that we had made this decision and vindicated it completely by showering us with affection. In the months that followed we became inseparable romping and playing and swimming and walking. There was no doubt in our minds that we had done the right thing.

Three months later we decided to make a film with Hercules, to be called "Hercules: Our Wrestling Bear". It was to be based around a typical day in his life.

After some investigations we finally fixed upon a company called Cinecosse and commissioned them to make the film. They had no idea

50 stone of bear is difficult to shift

what they were letting themselves in for, but they were delighted by the project, had an open mind and were ready for anything.

Herc immediately took over — unlike Andy and I who self-consciously bungled our parts for the first couple of days. He seemed to know exactly what was required, entertaining the film crew with a continual variety of comic antics and beautifully upstaging Andy in every scene. The Director, and his crew were delighted and within 24 hours had christened our big baby 'One take Herc'! Then came a hitch. Mike Marshall, the director wanted a wrestling scene as the centrepiece for the whole film. "It's crucial" he said, "Unless you want to completely alter the development of the movie and the title. You can't have a film called 'Our Wrestling Bear' without any wrestling in it!"

We explained the problem and said that it was impossible but he begged us to try it just once, since such was his faith in the hero of the film by this time that he was sure he would oblige.

I would have bet everything I had that Hercules would refuse to co-operate and Andy felt the same. After all, it had been so long and his dislike of the muzzle was too deep rooted. Andy approached the den with the thing in his hand and I waited for Hercules to back off in disgust. Then to his amazement the opposite happened. Up he came to his partner eager to begin the business of the day, which he was enjoying

'O.K. I submit'

enormously as it gave him lots of attention and rewards and involved very little work, and then down he sat and offered his big black nose to the muzzle!

We were astonished. All the way to the paddock where the cameras were waiting Andy shook his head in amazement, muttering "I don't believe it. I simply don't believe it."

Hercules acted as if nothing had happened at all and gave an expert demonstration of his prowess, and as I watched him I couldn't help but wonder what was going on in that complex brain of his. He quite clearly and voluntarily had offered to put up with something he detested in order to help us out of a tricky situation. I felt profoundly moved.

The end of the muzzle saga was the most moving incident of all. Indeed, it was a turning point in our whole relationship with our beloved boy. A turning point in the whole history of man's relationship with bears, come to that.

Two or three months after the film was made, Andy and Hercules had been on a long walk in the hills and were running and swimming down in the river near the Inn. Andy was walking in the shallows by the bank and Hercules was playfully ambling close behind him. Suddenly Andy slid on a stone and fell with a splash half on top of Herc. The latter immediately thought that his partner was starting another of their wrestling bouts, and seizing the opportunity to score points, jumped on Andy before he could get up, pinning him to the ground with his great bulk and jamming his huge snout into Andy's neck. The blood drained from Andy's face as he thought "Well this is it; he'll have my throat out now." Even had he wanted to he was utterly helpless under the great bulk of Hercules' stomach. The pair looked at each other seriously, and mutual understanding was heavy in the gap between their eyes. Then Hercules jumped up and backed off to allow Andy to get to his feet — quite out of character in a wrestling bout. He stood motionless, watched his precious friend and master as if to say "Have I made my point?"

Andy ran hell for leather up to the house, eagerly pursued by Hercules, burst into the kitchen with tears in his eyes and joy in his face. "THROW AWAY THAT MUZZLE, MAGGIE, WE'LL NEVER NEED IT AGAIN." I felt so proud of them both that I could have cried myself!

Starring roles

6 STARRING ROLES

Some five months before the World Record was broken in Perth, Hercules obtained his first advertising job.

The promoters of Hofmeister lager had seen a photograph of Herc in a newspaper and asked if we would consider doing a promotion tour for their product, since its trademark was a bear. It was our first opportunity to show Herules off south of the border and we accepted the job eagerly: we knew Hercules would do his stuff after the success of the premier in Edinburgh, and we had the bright new pick-up truck to take him down in.

There were to be five venues in all and the first was in Bournemouth. We drove down, towing a small wooden trailer full of provisions (the tour was going to last ten days) and were met by two representatives of the advertising agency and taken to the large night club where Hercules was to appear.

As we arrived at the stage door members of Suzy Quatro's band were unloading their gear: one of the roadies, glancing at Hercules as we led him in, said "Good suit that, innit, you can 'ardly tell the difference; looks really real . . ." He couldn't believe it when Hercules later turned out ot be the real thing!

At the door there was a large coloured bouncer in a smart blue suit waiting for the first opportunity to throw troublemakers out. He looked strong and fearsome, but when he saw Hercules come lumbering along he seemed to go a shade paler and dashed off howling "Man, Oh Man!"

The night club was very big, but the stage we had to use was tiny and almost covered with the promotional items. I hoped that the place wouldn't be too crowded, so that we could use part of the dance floor, but when I went onto the stage to introduce Andy and Hercules I was dismayed to see it packed with young people in vivid disco gear. The music was very loud and for a moment my nerves got the better of me, but the show must go on and I asked them to make less noise, other-

Bear Eats Man!

wise the bear they were about to meet would be scared off. Mercifully, they heeded my words, I think they believed they were going to see some sort of hoax!

Andy and Hercules came onto the stage, the former holding a juicy roast chicken to settle Hercules down with. You could have heard a pin drop as he considered the flushed faces peering at him in the semi-darkness while he munched his chicken. Then he relaxed and immediately started rolling on the floor: the audience were captivated and the girls started screaming as if he were a pop idol!

The rest of the tour went off without a hitch, although in Reading we had a bit of difficulty at our hotel . . . We were booked into Trust House Hotels wherever we went because they stood in their own grounds and there was plenty of greenery about. We were always given a ground-floor room so that we could back the truck right up to the window to reassure Hercules about his strange surroundings, and so that he could watch the television through our window. He is very fond of television, especially films that have a lot of action in them and cartoons (particularly 'Tom and Jerry')!

We were getting ready for bed and Herc was quietly watching the television through the window when a frustrated night manageress knocked on our door.

"There is a couple upstairs who are not happy about sleeping with a bear under their window. They say they can't sleep. Could you possibly have a word with them and reassure them that he will not climb up and eat them during the night?"

"Away up and speak to them Maggie, You're better at this sort of thing than I am," said Andy. The manageress nervously took me up to the room and then hid behind me. I understood her nervousness when the door was opened by a large and angry lady in curlers covered by a pink hairnet.

"I believe you're concerned about our bear," I began.

A bald headed man with spectacles, who had forgotten to put in his false teeth, came up behind her.

"Damned ridiculous," he hissed through his gums, "We've been here for three days now and haven't had a decent nights sleep yet, what with the workmen banging away from first thing in the morning and now this bloody bear beneath our window. A **bear**! I ask you!"

They were furious, and beyond reasoning with. We went back downstairs, and as the manageress left us she said "I hope Hercules will go to sleep now and not bump about, or I'll have to move you to another room."

As I got into bed I wondered what she could have meant. And then it started! Hercules had discovered that by rocking his cage he could make it clank against a roan pipe that ran past the angry couples' window and then when he clanked they came to the window to look daggers at him! He thought this was a great game and, although we told him to stop it, he was enjoying it too much, and after keeping quiet for a moment or two, started up again.

The couple had obviously gone to bed and were not coming to the window, for after rattling around for a time Hercules became desperate and started banging his heavy metal pot against the sides of the cage!

Later that summer we were contacted by the B.B.C., who were looking for a bear to take part in a film they were making for television, called "The Eagle of the Ninth". The plot of the film centred around the Roman legion that disappeared in Scotland and was about the son of the commander of the lost legion setting out to solve the mystery.

It was being shot at Fintry in Stirlingshire and the idea was to use Hercules in a scene where he would be fighting with wolves — done by trick photography of course. Two representatives of the B.B.C. came up to Sheriffmuir. As soon as they met Hercules and saw what he could

Gladiators

Bath-time on film

'I wonder what happens up here'

do, they changed the plan for the film and asked if Andy would take the part of a gladiator.

The day we were due to shoot the scene it poured with rain. We arrived at Fintry an met the rather miserable actors and film crews, and the director explained what he wanted. Everybody was cheered up by Hercules who rose to the occasion with his tricks and pranks in spite of the miserable weather, which he hates.

Then the rain stopped and we were ready to roll. The cameras and lights were set up: Andy was dressed up in a ridiculous gladiator's outfit with a hat with a big red feather in it: the actors all took their seats around the arena, and we were off.

Andy strode into the ring, followed by Hercules, who looked this way and that and didn't look very fierce to me. Then he reared up on his hind legs and went for the red feather! It looked very dramatic as Andy pretended to ward off the savage bear. They wrestled and tussled, and then the scene was over and Andy allowed Hercules to have the feather.

He contentedly rolled over on his back and proceeded to rip the thing to pieces. A plaintive voice cried from the watching crowd "Please someone, rescue my feathers!" But nobody was terribly keen to try! In the end Andy managed to prize them free with the help of some polo mint bribes.

The scene had gone so well that it did not require to be shot again. The actors and film crew were very impressed and gave my boys a standing ovation as the rain started again. No mean compliment from professionals: but then my men were professionals, too! Everybody dashed back to the buses and caravans to snatch a bite to eat and I asked Andy why he had been so flustered when he had come out of the make-up van at the start of the take.

He said that the two make-up men had fluttered about him like a couple of turtle doves, twittering about his strong muscles, slim hips, and so on, as they fitted him into his costume. The crisis came when they said he would have to wear a little leather loin cloth. He put it on but not to their satisfaction: "You'll have to take off your panties dear" They cried! Well what was a red-blooded Scotsman to do! Andy fled the van: I have never seen him look so bashful, and at the end of the take he flatly refused to go back to the van and I had to take his costume back and recover his clothes!

Another film we did with the B.B.C. was 'The Four Seasons' which was presented by David Bellamy. The series was about the history and development of plants. Apparently many seeds had come to this country at the end of the ice age when Britain was still attached to the continent of Europe, and many had been brought in the coats of animals such as bears who wandered about the land.

They wanted a brief scene to illustrate this and found a nice location at High Force waterfall in North Yorkshire. Hercules the Stone-Age bear was to wander up the stream towards the waterfall and find a salmon on a rock. The camera would watch him as he ate it up.

Andy told the director that Hercules would not eat raw salmon. "Nonsense," the director replied, "bears love salmon, and we have brought a beautiful fresh twenty pounder for him."

Sure enough, up came Hercules, looking every inch a wild bear, found the salmon, sniffed it disdainfully and left it where it was!

This was no good at all. What were they to do? Andy suggested that they leave a few tins of stone age 'John West tinned salmon' on the rock and in the end they slit open the salmon's belly and packed it with

'Good movie material, chasing horses . . .'

cooked fish! Up came Hercules, as before, and this time, after he had
sniffed the fish he ripped open its belly and guzzled all the cooked meat
inside. Once he had cleaned it out he tossed away the rest of the fish! I
don't know what the experts on bears diets who were watching the
programme must have thought!

By 1980 Hercules was very well known in Scotland from his
appearances at numerous events and from our touring around with our
film but as yet he was not very well known in the south, or abroad. It
was by chance that he was discovered for the role that would spread his
photograph into every city in the kingdom.

British Airways had embarked on an advertising campaign for
their 'poundstretcher' scheme which was based on using appropriate
animals to appear in the posters. To advertise the cheap fares to South
Africa, for example, they used an elephant; for Australia, a kangaroo;
and for Canada they needed a bear. The posters would show a fisherman and his son smilingly returning from a successful day on the river,
little realising that there was a grizzly bear, tip-toeing up behind them!

The South African and Australian projects had been realised without any great difficulty: the Canadian one was a different matter, however. The advertising agency had tried throughout the length and breadth of the U.S.A. and Canada to find a bear who could be safely taken under the lights of a photographic studio. Without success.

They were about to abandon the project when they heard that there was a bear in the Highlands of Scotland that might fill the bill.

We were contacted by a photographic studio near Edinburgh and confidently replied that Hercules could do the job.

'I can go over jumps too . . .'

'. . . but I prefer to go through them!'

The session took ten minutes! The photographer was amazed at how relaxed and assured Herc had been: he said it had taken him two days to get the picture he wanted of an elephant's trunk, and five hours to take a suitable picture of the fisherman and his son which was to be used with Hercules!

This project led directly to the biggest advertising scheme that Herc has been involved in to date, that for the Kleenex tissues — "The Big Softy" campaign.

The photographer who worked with us on the poundstretcher project was talking to a friend in the same business a couple of months later and asked what she was involved in at the moment.

"I'm working on this film for Kleenex" she said, "which features a lumberjack being wrestled by a bear. Impossible project. You don't happen to know any tame bears who might oblige?" She laughed. "As a matter of fact I do . . ."

Two days later she and two assistants arrived at Sheriffmuir from London. We had given her details on the telephone and told her that we were sure Hercules could do the job. She wanted to believe us, but it was clear when the southerners arrived that they doubted whether it would be possible.

Often when it was important for Hercules to give of their best he would rise to the occasion brilliantly and so it was that day. He proceeded to charm the pants off the Londoners with his good natured antics and obvious 'star quality'. 'The Big Softy' was born that day.

Having found a bear, the next thing was to find an actor to play the part of 'Hank', the lumberjack who is accosted by the bear in the advertisement. Andy was the obvious person for the part, both because of his relationship with Hercules and because of his physique, but because of the rules of Equity, the actors' union, the part would have to be auditioned in the usual way.

The part advertised required an actor to be attacked from behind by an almost full grown, nine foot tall, fifty-four stone grizzly bear. Five brave actors auditioned for the part. Each listened in disbelief as this was outlined to him by Robert, the enthusiastic director, and then withdrew their application. Andy would have to do the job himself, but to do this he would have to join Equity, usually a very long and difficult business involving having to work in a theatre for a couple of years.

As it turned out, the actors' union couldn't have been more help-

Big Hank grapples with the Griz

ful. So long as the proper forms had been filled in and the job duly advertised to their members, they had no objection to Andy joining, and thus being able to do the job.

We were due to arrive on location very early in the morning and drove there in the coach when it was still dark, arriving in time to meet Robert for an early breakfast. The site was in the middle of a large forest and it was a tricky job getting the bus there down the winding country lanes. Once we arrived, the brightly painted coach looked eerily out of place amongst the high trees. Technicians and film crew were arriving all the time — there seemed to be dozens of them in the gloom.

After breakfast we consulted with the wardrobe lady: I was reminded of Andy's previous brush with her profession! Here we immediately ran into difficulties. Although they had brought the biggest woodsman's shirts they could get, none of them were big enough. Indeed the first one they tried on my big man ripped down a seam as soon as he flexed his muscles. Although he pretended to be annoyed at this, in fact he was secretly proud of the fact that his biceps were substantially bigger than most mens! Here was a real problem: we could not put off the shooting to find a shirt, yet it would look strange if the lumberjack were working naked!

Just then a man who had been watching everything with keen interest stepped forward and said that he thought he could help. He disappeared for a moment and then returned with the perfect shirt for the job! He said he had been given it in Canada and wouldn't take anything for it.

After Andy's hair had been combed into a new style — he steadfastly refused to be made up! — we were ready to go and walked up a steep hill to where the filming was to be done. Earlier we had familiarised Hercules with the woods, so he felt quite at home as he walked with the rest of the crew. He seemed to sense that he was in for a bit of fun and the crew, although they had been wary to begin with, soon put their fears behind them. Throughout the rest of the time they spent filming they treated Hercules like a big Teddy bear, unperturbed as he walked among them occasionally bumping into their legs. "Oh sorry Herc," they would say, carrying on with their business as if it was the most natural thing in the world to have a grizzly bear running around their feet.

Bear on the loose

——7 BEAR ON THE LOOSE——

Fate has a mysterious way of threading itself through every life, and although we had been planning to take a holiday with Hercules on the Hebridean island of Benbecula for two or three years, we had for one reason or the other, never got around to it.

At the beginning of August, 1980 a convenient gap arose in our hectic schedule and we decided that the time for our much talked about holiday had arrived. Even so, it wasn't going to be a complete holiday as we intended to kill two birds with one stone. We would visit my mothers' family who came from the Islands and make a video film of Hercules, with the help of our friends Brian and June Davidson, as well as having a few days complete rest.

By the time we arrived on Benbecula we seemed to have put behind us months of feverish activity and although we had the video to make we felt more carefree than we had done in years. Perhaps Hercules sensed this, we'll never know — but he entered into a relaxed holiday mood with all his boisterous enthusiasm. No child can have been more thrilled with sea and sand, as Hercules was then.

Furiously inquisitive he would career over the dunes, leaping on the strange mounds of seaweed desperate to get into the sea and yet uncertain as to what would be there when he finally got in. He had never swam in sea water before and the new found buoyancy all went to show off his aquatic skills even more than usual. Time and again Hercules and Andy would charge into the sea like a pair of vast water babies, and with each dip Hercules would gain in confidence swimming with more grace and power, surging ahead as though driven by an expensive outboard motor. Should we have realised then what might happen? We didn't. We just watched, and laughed and felt as always, slightly awed by the power of this marvellous creature we were blessed with.

It was the third day of our holiday, and we were happier than we had ever been. Andy and Hercules, both impatient to get outside, went down to the sea for a pre-breakfast swim. I stood and lazily watched as the boys scrambled in and out of the water. It was tiring just watching them.

After half an hour Andy shouted "I think I'll bring him in now and give him his breakfast. If we stay in any longer we'll both be growing flippers!" I turned and walked back to the coach to get some beans to entice a reluctant Hercules out of the water when I heard Andy yell "Maggie, Maggie, — he's off. He's slipped his rope!" I turned to see Hercules thrusting his way through the water making for a small island nearby.

I froze. Andy and Hercules were now 70 feet apart and the gap was widening. Andy who was always so confident, so much in control, looked powerless, stunned, riveted in the shallows.

Hercules made the island, shook himself with regal nonchalance, and set of again in a northerly direction.

As luck would have it, Callum Macrae a local lobster fisherman, and his sons Donald and Duncan, came past in their small fishing boat. Andy snapped out of his shocked state and begged a lift to the far shore. The Macraes readily agreed, and I watched the small boat's agonisingly slow progress across the narrows. By this time Hercules had bounded to the top of the island and, without so much as a backward glance, had disappeared from sight.

After what seemed like an eternity, the Macrae's boat landed and Andy sprinted off in hot pursuit. I felt particularly helpless as all I could do was to stand and watch, but I was certain in my mind the worst that could happen was that the pair of them would be back for a late breakfast or alternatively an early lunch.

I waited and waited, pacing up and down the shore. Half an hour passed, 40 minutes — and then there was Andy shouting. There was an urgency in his voice and no Hercules lolloping by his side. Something was badly wrong.

"He's swimming across to the big island. Get the boat quick."

"Oh Lord" I blurted, knowing that for the first time since we had arrived we had left "Bearpower" in Lochmaddy instead of having her with us in case something awful like this happened.

Almost gabbling with panic, I grabbed Brian and June, and promising to explain what had happened en route, we set off at breakneck speed for Lochmaddy. Breakneck speed on the Hebrides, of course, is a different thing altogether from breakneck speed in Los Angeles — or

Stirling for that matter. Part of the charm of the islands is that everything happens infuriatingly slowly. As we drove to Lochmaddy I was inwardly screaming with frustration at the restriction of the single lane road, punctuated with passing places.

It was almost two hours since we had set off and I could feel a cold sweat developing at the thought of trying to launch the boat with the tide half out. Could we get the boat into the water, and, if we could, would the engine start?

Miraculously we got "Bearpower" into the water and started the engine. From there I steered through the channels, uncertain as to the exact direction we should be heading in, and worried that we would hit one of the many submerged rocks.

After 10 minutes we spotted Callum lifting creels on the east side of the big island. As we came alongside I shouted above the sputter of the outboard. "Andy still hasn't found Hercules — have you seen them?" I must have been a ridiculous sight as I was still wearing only a T-shirt, pink shorts and climbing boots, and Callum looking like an Old Testament prophet gave a look that was at once kind and reassuring but also mildly reproving as if to say "There's no point in getting panicked lassie".

"Don't worry" he said "They are on the island and Duncan is away to help Andy find Hercules. You've to wait here for them".

I felt reassured at once. It seemed as though I had over-reacted yet somehow I couldn't rid myself of a hundred and one nagging doubts. As we sat bobbing in the swell, scanning the island, I thought "What if Hercules was lost — really lost? What if the big soft lump were to be swept away in one of the fierce currents that surrounded the islands? What if through fear and disorientation he were to attack somebody?" As well as we both knew and loved Hercules, we only knew him with us, in a world that revolved around baked beans and grapes, order and warmth. Just how he would react on his own in the world was anyone's guess.

Suddenly, in the distance a figure appeared. Straining our eyes we made out Duncan who was waving frantically and pointing to the north-east end of the island.

"Just follow me and mind you dinna fall" said Callum, as we brought both boats into land. We hurriedly secured them and scrambled over the seaweed-covered rocks to the heathery cliff.

Duncan told us he thought that Hercules was still on the island

and we all set off, trampling through the heather. Like beaters, we walked in a line, shouting ourselves hoarse, but there was neither movement nor answer.

Nature seemed to be mocking us as we raised our feeble voices in shouts of "Here Herckie boy, Herc, Herc, Herc" — only to have the sounds muted by the vast sky and whipping wind.

My thoughts turned to poor brave Andy, as I watched the columns of grey rain clouds martial themselves on the northern side of the Island. It was getting darker and colder. I knew Andy had lost a shoe in the initial mad scramble and was only wearing a pair shorts.

Quite clearly we needed more help. It would soon be dark. We needed more eyes. I thought of the Army rocket range at Benbecula had passed the previous evening. Surely they would help.

I explained to the others my plan to recruit additional helpers and as we turned back to the boats, the heavens opened.

Amidst gusting winds and torrential rain we battered our way through by car to the base. We were met, well received, and escorted to the control tower, to see if it would be possible to take up the large blue and red Seaking helicopter that was parked at the side of the runway.

Despite the weather, we were soon airborne. I had never flown in a helicopter before and found myself caught up in the childish thrill of my first flight. When I was securely strapped in and my earphones were buzzing — the helicopter scythed its way through the wind to the part of the island where we thought Hercules might be.

Through the open side door, the view was superb. I began to feel more relaxed than I had since the moment Hercules had broken free as we swooped onto the island. As the pilot approached the area we had asked him to take us to — we spotted "Bearpower". The helicopter veered in the direction of the boat, and I spotted the familiar colours of Andy's red and blue tracksuit top. "Thank God he's got some clothes on at last" I thought. Feeling sure that he must be going back for Hercules, I agreed with the pilot that it would be best if we went back to base.

We were back on the ground within minutes, and having thanked everyone, we drove back to Petersport, never doubting that Andy would soon be back with Hercules tagging along behind him.

Through the darkness I heard the roar of a speedboat and my heart plummeted because I knew that if it was Callum himself the boat would not have been travelling at speed.

Once, when he was with us in "Bearpower" Callum had admitted that he never had travelled as fast in his life, not even in a car — almost as if to say that God has not intended man to travel at speed! And so I knew that Andy was alone in the boat — because Hercules, try as he might was far too big to get into it.

Andy threw me a rope to tie her up. I fired a flood of questions at him, only to be met by the untypically flat reply, "We'll get him in the morning".

As I walked up the pier, Andy who usually bounded everywhere shuffled beside me and told me in a tired hollow voice that he thought Hercules must have gone to sleep somewhere, exhausted after a day of constant running, and swimming through the strong currents, some of which measure up to nine knots.

Gradually we pieced together the fragments of the day's chase. Andy had lost all his zest, all his sparkle and he almost mumbled out the story of how after swimming the narrow channel Hercules had crossed the island and then without a second thought plunged in and started to swim the three-quarter of a mile through ferocious currents to the larger island of Wiay (pronounced Foo-Yae-EE).

Although in the peak of physical condition, as well as being a strong swimmer, Andy could only weakly watch from the top of the cliff, sure that Hercules would be swept away by the lethal current. His last sight of Hercules was of his brown head being buffeted by the waves as he swam towards Wiay.

Now the only possible way for Andy to catch Hercules was to cross over to Wiay by island-hopping, crossing each island on foot and swimming the stretches of water between them. Having lost his training shoe, his right foot was by now bleeding profusely, but still he kept on running over the harsh heather and swimming the murderous narrows, always just too far behind and yet always convinced that he would round a corner, receive a mighty pat on the shoulder and be set upon by his wrestling partner in a bout of mischievousness.

Hours passed and still Andy could find no sign either of Hercules, or of Duncan, who had come to help him and was scouring other parts of the island.

When they met up with each other in the evening it was Duncan, ironically enough, who had sighted Hercules from the peak of the hill. But knowing that he could not easily get to Hercules, and that even if he could he probably would be unable to control him, he had doubled back to search for us, hoping that Hercules would not move too far away from the spot.

After I had heard the story, and seen how exhausted Andy was and examined the extent of the cuts on his foot, we both agreed that he must rest and that we would set off again at first light.

We both knew that Hercules would be scared. It was his first night alone since he had come to us, but we also knew that, desperately though we wanted to, we were both too exhausted to continue the hunt, while the islands, hazardous enough by day, would be suicide by night, pocked as they are with bogs and crevasses.

'Keep your eyes peeled, men'

'He's here somewhere'

'Here Herc,' calls Sergeant Anderson,
'Here Hercie Boy'

Friday morning dawned at last to end a lonely night. We had both slept badly, missing desperately that familiar rumbling and snoring from the back of the coach.

We were up at the crack of dawn and Andy and Brian headed straight for Wiay. June and I waited for the soldiers from the base who had volunteered their help.

The soldiers, sixty in number, arrived at 6.30 a.m. and we set off in convoys, each convoy split into 2 search parties taking a different starting point on the island and working its way inland.

I was with the group that included the very cheerful policeman Sgt. Anderson, a tower of strength, who was to be so kind to us over the coming weeks. Despite my anxiety, I couldn't help smiling at Sgt. Anderson's calls of "Here Herkie boy, Herc boy", as if he were looking for a puppy, or coaxing a kitten out of a tree. If Hercules had risen in front of him, to his full eight feet in height he would have fainted!

We trudged on. My legs were aching from yesterday's exertions, and it always seemed to be a struggle to get through the dense heather. The fact that I was carrying Andy's bag filled with beans and meat didn't make my life any easier. I was constantly slipping and stumbling like a Saturday night drunk.

As the day wore on, and the crackling reports on the soldiers walkie/talkies made it apparent that the other groups were having as little success as we were — I began to cry inwardly from exhaustion and fear.

I just couldn't understand it. It was so unlike our boy. He was always rushing to and fro in his eagerness to find out what was over the next hill.

"Oh please God where are they?" I prayed, as my eyes filled with tears. I spotted Andy. Someone was running towards him. My heart thumped, and I rushed forward I knew they had found him. "Have you seen him?" I shouted, "They have found some prints over there", Andy said pointing to the North.

We all trudged behind the two soldiers who had seen his prints. "If his prints are there, surely he can't be too far away" I said "Keep your fingers crossed babe" said Andy, who seemed close to tears himself.

The sun was blazing down and I was relieved of my burden of beans and meat. We reached the peaty patch where the soldiers had found the two tracks. Having closely examined them Andy said "Well that proves he has been here", but I think we all doubted what we saw. After almost two days of searching we had come across two prints — no more, because the peat patch was small and surrounded on all sides by heather. The two big paw marks seemed to start and end from nowhere, just as though Hercules had been whisked away into thin air.

We spread out and searched all round the area, but no other prints were found, the only movements coming from a group of puzzled sheep who looked surprised to see their sunny day disturbed.

Searching seemed futile in this barren wilderness of peat bogs and heather. Heather, that simple hardy plants much loved by tourists who stick it in tweed caps and car radiators was a stubborn foe that seemed to blur the vision in a mist of browns and purples — disguising valleys and hills alike.

We had all been on the island for almost seven hours. The further we went the greater our task seemed to be. Knowing that we could not ask again for the helicopter from the base, as it was needed for secret testing in the North Sea, I suggested to Andy that we hire one. He agreed, but said that he would stay on the island to continue searching on foot.

It was 2 pm, and for the second time in two days I was driven to the airstrip. Once there, we were told that it would take the helicopter an hour-and-a-half to arrive from Glasgow.

I couldn't find the energy to speak. I sat waiting, staring blankly ahead of me, trying to keep the fears back, and saying my private prayers in the hope that God would let us find our boy, my baby.

The control tower filled with people, police, press, army and my old friend Eddie Orbell from the wildlife park at Kingussie, where Hercules was born. Seeing the sympathetic look in Eddie's eyes as he said in his soft southern accent "We'll get him for you Maggie, he's out there somewhere", a lump came into my throat, and I had to swallow hard and grit my teeth to stop myself crying.

Minutes were like hours. I kept my eyes averted from everyone, knowing that I had to keep calm, knowing that I had to stop my boiling emotions from spilling over, as I had to try to be alert in order to be able to go up in the helicopter and try and spot Hercules.

Eventually the helicopter landed outside the control tower. After a few minute's delay for a fuel check, I was aboard, strapping myself in and securing the mike. The rotor blades roared above us, and we were airborne.

We swept over Wiay, back and forth, back and forth, methodically combing the island, section by section, down to only a matter of feet above the ground if we saw something we thought was moving or might possibly be Hercules.

My head ached with the buzz of the headphone and I thought my eyeballs would burst out of their sockets with the strain of looking so hard.

We had four pairs of eyes, my own, the pilots and Brian and June's. But still we could see nothing, except sheep who remained calm despite the roar of the helicopter. But Hercules could not be seen.

"I think we should try the mainland of Benbecula itself now", I told the pilot, "He may have swam back over there".

We could fly even lower over the ground on the flat stretches of Benbecula. But our search of the mainland proved just as fruitless as our search of Wiay. As we swept over the bogs and neatly stacked piles of peat, the crofters would wave as if to wish us well. All the islanders seemed to know what was happening, as nothing remains a secret in the Hebrides for long.

When we returned to the airport we were greeted with official cars and what seemed like hundreds of stern uniformed men.

Perhaps it was my imagination but these grim-faced men seemed just as worried as ourselves, already bound up in our agonizing adventure, and no doubt worrying whether Hercules would lay waist to the islands.

I stepped from the helicopter shaking my head with disbelief. "There's no sign of him at all, if he had been moving we would have seen him" I said. Andy looked at me, his face drawn with worry, it was as if we were both caught in an unending nightmare, with nothing seeming to be as it should have been. Everyone surrounding us seemed remote, we were floating, totally lost. Andy put his big strong arms around my shoulder and said "He must still be on the island, we just haven't looked in the right place that's all". It was finally all too much for me and I openly wept like a baby.

We called off the search for that day and went back to the coach to eat and sleep determined to search Wiay again in the morning. This time we would use more soldiers and tracker dogs brought over from Skye. Surely we would find him tomorrow.

The Third Day

After another night when we both seemed to be more often awake than asleep, we started our search again. We tried to give each other new hope, saying how the tracker dogs must be able to help, and how Hercules must by now be ravenously hungry and on the lookout for food which would surely make him easier to find.

But we were both nagged by awful unspoken doubts, not wanting to depress each other even further. We both knew that Hercules had not run away from us, but in playing a game and thrilled with the new found buoyancy of the sea, he had swum too far. Now he was lost and frightened and in attempting to get back to us, he might actually be going further away.

Daylight brings comfort in the same strange way that darkness turns the mind to imagining the blacker side of things, and so we did not set out in an entirely hopeless state.

In due course the army arrived in a convoy of buses and land rovers. The tracker dogs were not far behind them. The three dogs were unloaded from blue vans by their handlers.

It was not long until we were on Wiay again and we once more divided into groups. It surprised me that the handlers did not want any piece of clothing with Hercules' scent on it — but they assured me that the dogs would pick up any strange smell. I crossed my fingers and nodded, presuming my preconceptions about tracker dogs to be wrong, but silently doubting that the dogs could pick up Hercules' subtle, almost non-existent woody scent.

I stayed with the middle group and a black alsatian who looked keen to start. Together with a soldier with a walkie/talkie set connected to base we set off into the wind.

Although I was once again carrying my bag of food, ready to run to the scene at the first hint of a sighting, walking was much easier that day, as we kept to the higher ground, avoiding the peat marshes.

The dogs stayed out in front so that any strange scent might not be confused with our own. We tried to keep them in view at all times, but this proved impossible. The lie of the land was such that dogs and handlers were constantly disappearing from view.

My eyes were by now becoming accustomed to the constant slow sweeping searches I carried out through the high powered binoculars. I took in every dark object and concentrated hard on it in order to identify exactly what it was.

We started our search on the south side of the island and worked our way northwards to where Duncan last sighted him, on the first day.

When we had been walking for two or three hours I heard a shout and turning saw the soldier to my right was sunk to his waist in the bog. He was sinking fast and each movement he tried to make only took him deeper. I realised that I had to act quickly and removed my jacket. Edging towards the boggy patch, I threw the sleeve to him. He caught it and within a minute I had managed to work him free. He was visibly shaken, and, as he was wiping himself down, said "I hope Hercules didn't do what I did." "I hope not", I replied, not wanting to hurt the soldier's pride by telling him that Hercules was far too sensible and too cautious to go blundering into a bog! Hercules would never tread on anything if he suspected the ground might give way: he might come to the edge of a bog, but his quick mind and strong instinct for self-preservation would prevent him from going any further, and he would tread warily until he had found a better route to take.

"Aren't You Glad We Didn't Go To France, Dear ? — You Don't Get Blockaded Up Here In The Hebrides"

Presented to HERCULES
by the members of The Cartoonists' Club of Great Britain
who voted him GOLD JOKER of 1980

By the end of the third day we were cold and disappointed

When we finally climbed to the top of the highest peak on Wiay we could watch the dogs on both sides of us and had a much better idea of what was happening. I caught sight of Andy at the east side of the island and saw him drop disconsolately to the ground. I wished then that he was up on top of the hill with me, to offer me comfort and be comforted in return. The dogs had neither seen nor smelt anything unusual and after another hour I went over to join Andy to see if he had found any traces of our lost boy.

All hope gone

I could see the disappointment written over Andy's broad sun-tanned face. He and Archie had found another couple of footprints but nothing else. Once again the prints had disappeared into thin air, as though someone was playing a cruel game with us, building up our hopes only to dash them again.

We decided to search in the direction the footprints were leading, so we made for the north-east of the island, searching every crack as we went in the hope of finding more prints or some, any, kind of lead.

The rest of the soldiers, had by now started to head southward and would be coming to the end of their search. It seemed that we were all looking in completely the wrong places, since there were any number of small islands he could have swum to in his panic.

For the third day we had to admit defeat. My legs felt as if I would never walk again and although Andy's physical strength had not deserted him — he was utterly frustrated mentally. If the islands themselves knew where Hercules was hiding, they were not willing to yield their secrets.

Back at Petersport we were met by hordes of press men and photographers, all anxious to learn if we had any news. I had nothing to say, I could only think of myself and could not find a single word to express how I felt. The day seemed a dismal repetition of the day before and the day before that. Andy tried to put a brave face on it, saying "He's out there watching us all. He's probably sitting behind a rock, feet up, thoroughly enjoying his holiday". His replies brought a chorus of laughter amidst the gloom. Perhaps the press could not notice, as I could, how much Andy's voice was tingling with sadness, and that, even though he was hiding his anguish well, it would not take much to bring my mighty man to his knees.

I sat in a corner of the coach, my eyes sore and puffy, staring into space. I knew that everyone meant well and I could see the affection and concern they felt for Hercules, but it did not ease the pain.

Later that night Andy Higgins of the Daily Mail came to the coach and with tears in his eyes said "I would willingly give a million pounds and give up my job if I could help you get Hercules back I'm so sorry."

"If only he was here to see how much everybody loved him", I thought and dropped my head into my hands, trying to hide my tears.

After everyone had gone and we were alone again, Andy sat looking longily at the island, as if by staring long enough and hard enough Hercules would simply appear and the nightmare would be over.

He turned to me, his eyes looking tired and bloodshot, "They think he's drowned, don't they". I nodded. He turned away and I saw his shoulders heave. The dam had burst and his tears flowed, but, even in front of me, he was still trying to hide his tears. I knew only too well how he felt and wanted to tell him to let it all out, but the words seemed to stick in my throat. He got up and walked down to the end of the pier. I could only stare hopelessly at his broad back and pray once more that this nightmare would end.

On the edge of despair

Disappointment after disappointment

We ate some supper that night, not from hunger, but from the realization that we had to keep up our strength to be able to keep searching. The food went down, but tasted of nothing. That night was the worst yet. Our nightmare was becoming a reality: it was happening, and the empty room at the back of the coach was the glaring proof of it all.

Peace would not come that night, even though every one of my muscles ached with tiredness. Once again I lay awake staring at the sky, trying to doze intermittently only to wake once more.

Andy had withdrawn into himself. The only thing in his life that he felt no embarrassment over demonstrating his love had vanished. I awoke in a sweat to find him turned away from me, his body wracked with sobs. In the darkness his tears had found an outlet. I turned and bit the pillow as I tried to muffle the sound of my own tears, thinking how two people normally so close can suddenly through necessity shut each other out, by trying not to make the other any more unhappy through their own sadness.

The Fourth Day

The fourth day dawned wild and blustery, the rain beating a tattoo on the roof of the coach. Until now the weather, with the exception of the wind and rain on the first day, had been fair — and my thoughts turned to Hercules and to how he hated the rain, preferring in bad weather to stay lying in his den listening to music that filtered through from the kitchen or the bar, and only venturing out to see if the day looked like brightening up.

The previous evening Duncan had told us, not meaning to worry us further but to ensure that the fullest possible search was made, that there were 12 large hidden crevasses on the island of Wiay. These were not easy to find, and known only to the local shepherds and fishermen. They were covered by a thick layer of heather, and hence invisible to the eye, but once the heather was parted, or any real pressure placed on it, the ground fell away in a sheer drop some 150 feet to the sea below. He thought it best that we checked these crevasses to see if Hercules had fallen into one of them.

Although we knew Hercules to be cautious, we realised that there was the chance of him having made some ghastly mistake and so we resolved to spend the day checking the crevasses, and rechecking the small lochs on the centre of the island. We could not rule out any possibility — and we were haunted by the thought that Hercules might be lying suffering at the bottom of a gully or crevasse.

The day started along the now familiar lines. Once we had split into groups, we began to comb the island again.

That day I was walking with an islander called Davie Shepherd who was always ready with a smile and encouragement, and would produce endless sweets from a large bag he carried with him. Davie was full of theories as to where Hercules could be and we tried them one by one, finishing with the crevasses which was no easy task. After that we had exhausted even his fertile imagination.

We went on to search all the tiny islands surrounding Wiay. Each one, small though it might be, had to be thoroughly investigated for we were determined to leave no stone unturned.

During the afternoon the seas mounted, and we had to stick close to the coast. As we made our way back to Petersport, the fishermen who were with us started to talk of the Minch, the formidable stretch of water between the Inner and Outer Hebrides, famed for being one of the most unpredictable in the British Isles. They talked of how the treacherous currents had claimed many fishing boats, and, though they did not say so, it was clear they felt that Hercules might have made for the only visible land mass — Skye on the other side of the Minch.

On a clear day, such as it had been when Hercules first disappeared, the cliffs of Skye were just visible on the horizon.

My secret feeling was that Hercules had far too much common sense to think he could swim that far. I just couldn't believe he had set off into the wild blue yonder.

In the four years since we had brought Hercules home from the Wildlife Park at Kingussie we had time and again marvelled at his common sense. Once, when we were at Loch Earn and Hercules was out swimming with us, he started to swim across the loch. When he had gone almost a third of a mile he started back, seeming to realise that he might not get to the other side safely. Andy and I had always remarked to each other, like two proud parents, that where everything else would perish, Hercules would survive.

Surely he could not have lost all his common sense in a few days, and thrown his life away without a thought? No, not my Hercules. With this thought, which Andy, of course, shared, we decided that, somewhere Hercules was still alive — the big question was where?

That night we decided, having asked our friends in the Press to publicise it for us, that we would offer a reward of a thousand pounds to the first person who sighted Hercules, on the understanding that the sighting must lead to his recapture.

The Fifth Day

For the first time since we lost Hercules, I had a decent night's sleep. Whether it was through sheer fatigue or not I didn't know, but I woke only once on that windy night, and snuggled into Andy who was asleep like a log beside me.

The local gamekeepers had sent word to us the previous evening that they would like to try and help us find Hercules. Not only did they offer their own services, but those of their dogs and we were only too glad to accept their help. Grateful though we were, the tracker dogs had been no use, but the gun dogs were used to driving into deep heather to retrieve game, and so they might be of real help in raising a sleeping Hercules. The heather was so dense that it would be possible to pass within feet of him and miss him, since his coat would blend perfectly with the natural surroundings — just as nature intended.

True, it was a slim chance that Hercules would be sleeping in the wild during the day, but it was another possibility that we could not overlook, since the freak events of the past few days may have triggered off his hibernation cycle.

In the wild hibernation normally is a gradual process that happens to bears during the late autumn months when food begins to run short and the weather is deteriorating. The bear's body then produces a drug which enters the blood stream and it begins sleeping for increasingly long periods of time until full hibernation is reached.

It was only late August and still relatively warm in the Hebrides, and so it was unlikely that Hercules would have drifted into this state, but perhaps hunger and the shock of being lost had made him hide and, in turn, sleep.

There was no food on the islands, other than shellfish on the shore and sheep. Although Hercules ate only cooked food, the possibility that he might try to kill a sheep had, of course entered our heads, but that would be foreign to his whole upbringing. If he was in the wild long enough, we had no doubt that he would learn to kill — that is, if he didn't starve to death first — but, as it was, he was only used to running in the field with the sheep at home. There he had caught them only to get a sniff of them. Then he had let them run away, and the worst they had suffered was a slight shock.

Hercules always went out of his way not to hurt anything, even the month old kitten he had trapped under his massive paws received no more than a loving lick from the gentle giant.

When we started out on the day's search I was aching all over, stiff with the last few days' exercise as well as suffering a lot of pain from a back injury I had received falling from a horse earlier in the summer.

The tweed-clad keepers were prompt and their dogs, which at first I thought looked too old for a full day's work, were more than up to the job. They were eager and obedient, diving into the undergrowth and popping up every now and then as if to make sure that they were keeping their masters happy.

Andy and I watched from a few paces behind, and walked silently for most of the day, ever hopeful that the enthusiastic retrievers would raise Hercules from his slumber.

Yet again the island yielded nothing and as we took the now familiar way back to the boat, the awful doubts began to set in again.

We had now eliminated all the obvious and not so obvious hiding places, had covered in one way or another every nook and cranny of Wiay and we were still without a single clue, other than the two sets of isolated footprints.

Somehow Andy was managing to put on a brave face for all the well-wishers who continually appeared in Petersport to show their concern and offer suggestions as to where Hercules might be.

Everyday the papers were full of news. The Cartoons of Hercules drinking with his new Highland neighbours would have been funny, but for the seriousness of the whole situation. Headlines reading HERCULES BEATS THE ARMY or HERCULES TAKES A BREAK FROM STARDOM stared out of practically every paper in the country, with even the *Sunday Times* giving him front page billing.

"If only he were here to see it" I sighed, picturing his great big gentle head and soft brown eyes.

The Sixth Day

Tuesday, the sixth day since Hercules had gone missing, arrived. The weather continued to be bad and the spring tides were running. Bankrupt of ideas, we decided that Andy should visit South Uist as it was just conceivable that Hercules might have reached there by crossing the flats at low tide and swimming where it was necessary.

It was agreed that I should stay at the coach in case Hercules should be spotted, and needless to say that, desperately though I wanted to find him, I welcomed the opportunity to rest.

There was not a trace of Hercules on South Uist, and it was totally unrealistic to imagine we had a hope of finding him should he be there, unless he was accidentally sighted or we had several thousand men to search it from top to bottom. The mountains were steep and pitted with small caves and gullies, a climbers' paradise but a searchers' nightmare.

Our hopes were wearing very thin. We felt that all we could do now was to sit and wait for someone to spot our boy. It was stalemate. Our conversations were becoming less and less frequent and more stilted, as we each brooded over our unspoken thoughts and fears.

Just as we had reached the point when our morale was at breaking point, we received good news. A pilot from Stornoway on the Island of Lewis contacted us to say that he would fly us over the islands.

It was just what we needed. In a light plane we could scan the difficult terrain much more thoroughly than on foot, and I rang him that evening to accept his kind offer. He agreed to fly down the next morning if the weather was suitable. Once again the pain in my heart seemed to ease a little, with renewed hope for tomorrow.

The Seventh Day

The next day I was eager to be off as soon as possible. Brian and June, who had only come to make a video of Hercules and who had been unwittingly caught up in the whole drama, were going home. Not driven with the same compulsion as ourselves, nor as physically fit, they were completely exhausted. The daily searching had punished us all, and as they struggled to secure the tow bar of the caravan to the ball coupling on their car, they looked desperate to get away from the intricate nightmare Andy and I were plunged in. We would miss them because they had been with us from the very start.

However, Andy and I could not get away from our nightmare so easily. My mind kept saying over and over again, "If only we had gone somewhere else, if only . . ." But we couldn't leave, we had to go on.

Brian was going to give me a lift to the airport, and as I climbed into his car binoculars in hand, Andy shouted "I'm going over to Wiay again. I've a funny feeling that he is still there. I'll see you when you get back." Confusion was written all over his weary unshaven face. He just couldn't take it all in: refusing to admit to the full reality of Hercules' disappearance seemed to be Andy's passport to sanity in a world turned upside down.

Once at the airport and having said goodbye to Brian and June I telephoned the pilot, Bob Ford-Sangers. He said that the conditions were too hazy, but that if I could wait at the airport he would phone back as soon as he felt visibility was improving. Of course, I agreed, and waited six hours, drinking endless cups of tea and coffee.

The day did not clear up, and eventually Morag, an assistant to the controller, called a taxi for me. Once again I felt completely useless, a pawn in a game over which nobody — least of all me — had any control.

When I got back to Petersport I was confronted with a rare sight. Andy was smiling. My heart leapt and I felt my stomach churn. At last, it must be good news.

As I stepped out of the car, Andy beamed at me and said "I found his collar. I knew he had been to the island for a while. I just knew it. Quick get the kettle on and we'll have a cup of tea — he's over there somewhere sleeping. I just know it".

This was the old Andy I had almost forgotten, smiling and jabbering away nineteen at least to the dozen . It was the quickest cup of tea I've ever had — it went down in seconds — and once again we were off.

Wiay seemed to hold the key to the mystery. Perhaps the island was ready to give up her secret, for today, as we made the crossing, even the sea seemed friendlier, the lapping of the waves gentler.

I ran and half walked to keep up with Andy, laughing happily at the thought of all three of us reunited again, being able to return together to our familiar routine at Sheriffmuir.

We reached the place where Andy had found Hercules' collar, and it gave a sudden injection of hope. We had been searching the island for a week and had passed the spot literally a hundred times.

Standing on the path looking downwards to a small loch, I noticed the heather and ferns at the very edge of the water below were flattened, as if they had been trodden on. I slid down the banking and landed in a perfect den. It was completely hidden, commanded a panoramic view, and was embedded in the very side of the loch at water level camoflaged by an overhanging roof of peat and ferns. The sides were scooped out to give it walls, and a layer of soil and ferns at least six inches deep made a comfortable mattress. To the front was a small row of slim-stemmed rowan trees, which prevented anyone from looking into the den, but which allowed the inhabitant a perfect view. It was definitely Hercules's — it carried all his trademarks.

"He must have spent at least one night here, maybe more", I said excitedly, delighted with my find.

"I'm sure he's on this island somewhere" Andy kept repeating, as we set off again to look at all the really deep lochs. We had searched them all before, but some were so steeply banked that we had not gone right down to the water's edge. On this occasion we intended to do a much more thorough job.

Many of the lochs were so steep that Andy had to swim round them, while I scrambled along the sides, the bag of food cutting into my shoulders and all the while being mercilessly bitten by the midges that abounded in the clammy heat of the lochsides.

I watched Andy swimming below me, peering into every ledge, missing nothing, leaving nothing to chance. We managed to thoroughly search four large lochs and several small ones that afternoon, before the intense cold of the dark peaty water forced Andy to retire for the day, his body a kaleidoscope of blue, purple and white blotches. Tomorrow, we would return, equipped with wet suits.

The Eighth Day

I woke early with the coach being buffeted by a strong wind, and turning to look at the sleeping Andy wondered how long his strength could last. Letting Andy go on sleeping, I thought of the events of the last cruel week, and wondered what the outcome would be.

I still could not really believe Hercules had gone, and looking at his empty den at the back of the bus, I thought of him looking at me, scolding me for not having got out of bed sooner to make his normal gallon of tea.

Andy stirred, and turned towards me saying nothing, but knowing immediately how I was feeling. Each day we woke in hope and when darkness fell we were left alone with our despair and frustration. As we constantly tried to put ourselves in Hercules' position, imagining what he would do, we knew that at best we were only wildly guessing. Of course, our doubts as to whether Hercules was still alive had grown, but still we stubbornly refused to accept even the possibility.

I made a good large breakfast for us that day, knowing that, unless the weather improved drastically, the plane would be unable to make the crossing from Stornaway and so that we would have to continue our search of the lochs.

Both wearing wetsuits, I combed the higher edges of the lochsides while Andy continued his marathon swims around the lochs.

The day began to brighten up, and my wetsuit, which had been a blessing when we started out in the cold wet morning, became a curse.

Even after I had unzipped the jacket the heat was unbearable. My legs and back were excrutiatingly painful, and after I had stumbled over the heather for the umpteenth time, tears of rage, frustration and utter disappointment filled my eyes. As I lay sobbing I realized that I just could not go on and passed the point of no return. Andy knelt down beside me and took me in his arms.

"I think we'll go back now. I'll come back later on, there are only two more lochs to do."

I knew he was trying to spare my feelings and let me off the hook so I got up and stumbled down the hill with him.

As we were mooring the boat back at Petersport we heard a buzzing overhead and looked up to see a small yellow and white plane circling over the island. Bob had managed to fly down after all.

We watched for a while and then walked back to the coach. There we learned that Archie the taxi driver, who was one of our army of helpers, had twice come down to the port trying to contact us, and, failing to do so, had gone up in the plane with Bob to act as the second pair of eyes.

I flopped into one of the chairs on the coach and had just closed my eyes for a second, when Andy put his hand on my shoulder and said, "Maggie, I think you should go to the airport. There's no sense in them flying over the island any more, so get the control tower to tell Bob to start searching the mainland."

There now seemed little real hope that we would ever find Hercules. Andy was by now at the lowest I had ever known him. Like a drowning man clinging to wreckage he refused to let go of the idea that Hercules was still alive. He had done everything humanly possible, had driven himself beyond his physical limits and further. He could find nothing to say, nothing to suggest but he was staying "by God he was, until he knew either way".

Words just seemed to make it worse. I spent hours trying to reason with him that he had done all he could, and finally I persuaded him to fly home with me. He could leave the coach with my uncle

Archie, and if Hercules was sighted we could be back up on the island within an hour-and-a-half.

It was while we were packing that the awful finality of what we were doing began to sink in. We were leaving without Hercules.

We had one last farewell to make at my uncle's house on Grimsay — and it was there that fate chose to take another cruel turn.

When we arrived at my uncle's house, my aunt Effie, a primary school teacher, said that she had heard an odd story at school that day. On arriving at school the children had been full of gossip about the carcass of a sheep being stolen. I saw Andy's face light up as he waited eagerly to hear the rest of the story.

Effie went on to tell that "seemingly in a stretch of land called Eochar on the island of South Uist, a crofter had had his barn door broken in, a sheep carcass torn in two, and half of it stolen. It sounded just the sort of thing he might do — especially if, as he must have been, ravenously hungry.

On hearing the news Andy immediately asked my uncle Archie to telephone around to see if there was any truth in the story. After a few phone calls we learned that "yes the story was true".

Archie drove us hastily to Eochar, to the rather rundown croft of a Mr. McQueen, but had warned us on the way not to expect too much as the man had a reputation for telling tall tales.

We arrived at the house and were met by two young men, who showed us the shed where the carcass had been hanging. The door was indeed off its hinges.

Andy and I looked at one another, shaking our heads and not wanting to expect too much, but, as always, any small spark quickly kindled the fires of hope inside us.

The shed was old and had a thatched roof. We had a good look inside and tried to visualise what Hercules would have done in the situation. We both agreed, laughing, that he would have been extremely sneaky, practically tiptoeing out of the shed, having first peeped round the corners to make sure the coast was clear.

Andy told the young men that he would have to inform the police and get the search going again. The dark headed one who slouched with his hands in his pockets said, keeping his eyes firmly fixed on the floor, "You'll have to tell the old man first". "Where is he?" replied Andy eager to get going.

"He'll be down in Cregory," said the spokesman with his eyes still averted. "We'll get him for you, just wait here," and the pair walked away looking most unhappy about the whole affair.

After half an hour there was still no sign of the old man. We were thinking perhaps the bird had flown the coop.

At last a car drew up and what was clearly 'the old man' got out.

"Hello there" said Andy, "Can we talk about the door being knocked down?"

"Yes, but if the police come I'll say that I knocked the door down. You see, the boys might get into trouble for having the carcass hanging in the shed in the first place."

The lonely road home

An empty den

"That's fine with me" said Andy, being only interested to learn anything he could tell us about Hercules.

'The old man' told us how he had never seen anything like it in his life, and he drew a diagram on the steamed-up car window of how he had discovered the carcass torn in two.

"I'm not saying it was your bear mind" he said, "but it would take a phenomenal strength to do it — it couldn't have been a dog and I don't want to tell you no lies, but I've never seen nothing like it."

He sat silently smiling, waiting for an answer.

"Did you see any unusual paw marks?" Andy said, looking him straight in the eye. The old man pushed his cap further up on his head, and scratched his temple with a nicotine-stained finger.

"Well there may have been, and there may not have been" he replied enigmatically. "What I saw" he continued "was more a sort of group of wee circles each about an inch and a half in diameter, and to our delight they resembled Hercules's.

"Now, I'm telling you no lies" he said, looking sternly at us both.

"That's what I saw."

Andy and I were convinced, and, although the old man looked a bit of a wag, we believed him. It all seemed to fit.

Once back at my uncle's house we telephoned the police, but instead of receiving the news enthusiastically they were extremely sceptical as to the validity of the story because it had come from old McQueen, but they said they would look into the matter just the same.

Our plans to go home the next day were put to one side, as we promised each other that, if it had been Hercules who had taken the carcass, we would search the area until we found him.

Having been in the depths of depression only six hours earlier, we went to bed that night more cheerful than at any time since Hercules had gone missing and, after eating a delicious supper cooked by Aunt Effie, we went to bed and were asleep in seconds.

I awoke next morning with Andy's arms around me. He kissed me and said "Well Babe, let's hope things look as promising this morning as they did last night." I nodded, and silently prayed that he was right.

I telephoned the police station straight after breakfast and asked to speak to Sgt. Anderson. I was told that he had been out at Eochar since the early morning and I was given a number there. My lips were dry with anticipation as I dialled the number.

"Hello, may I speak to Sgt. Anderson please?" I said. "Yes. Just one moment", came a voice from the other end. Sgt Anderson came to the phone.

"It's Maggie Robin, Sergeant," I began, "What do you think, it's just like Hercules would do isn't it?" I had no doubt that he would agree and I could visualise telephoning the army to tell them that the search could be resumed on the strength of the new evidence. His answer stunned me.

"No Maggie, I'm afraid not. Of course I don't know the bear as well as you, but we have thoroughly searched the area and can't find any evidence of him having been there. I'm very sorry. I know how disappointed you must be."

"What about the door, the carcass?" "I know it's hard, Maggie, but between you and me we are ninety per cent certain it was a human animal that broke the door and stole the carcass, if you know what I mean."

I couldn't believe what he was saying, nor believe that all our rekindled hope could vanish in a few seconds.

Despite Sgt. Anderson's devastating news we decided that we should search the area in case the police had missed something.

Somehow we dragged ourselves through the next two days, as we scoured the beaches and dunes, oblivious to the beautiful scenery, and intent only on finding some clue that would say our boy was still alive.

It was late on that bleak Wednesday evening that we finally made the decision to go home, we had not so much run out of places to look but in the vastness of the desolate stretches of land, we did not know where to start.

It would take years to search every peaty bog and even then, who could be sure that we would cover the spot where our boy was lying.

We had to admit defeat, at least for the time being, the elements of nature had pitted her wits against us and had been returned the victor. A mighty adversary indeed.

All the goodbyes had been said, all the thank yous had been given, amidst the nightmare we had found friendship and comradeship that came only from the sincerity of the heart. The islanders had taken us into their lives and shown us kindness that could not be measured in depth, and a kinship that grew from the fact that they lived their lives needing each other. Nothing was asked in return.

We had come to the islands with our lives full, a happy threesome, delighting in the pleasure we found in each others company, but now the vital link was missing, we had lost our boy. Those cheeky eyes that saw all, the bright mind that missed nothing, it was all gone . . .

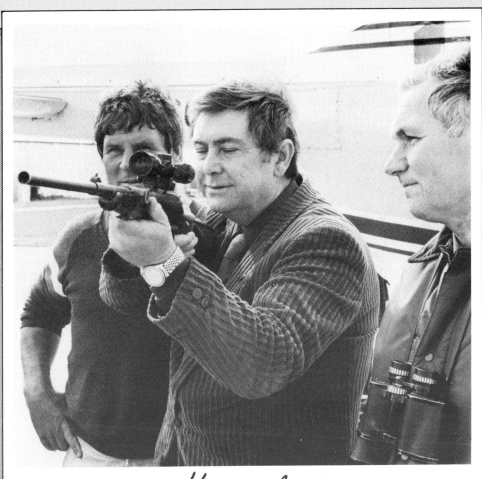

Home at last

———8 HOME AT LAST———

On the fourteen-hour journey home here we spoke only a few words to each other. In Andy's haggard face I saw the reflection of my own sorrow, coupled with a look of total defeat. I knew that when we reached the brow of the hill, just before the white walls of the Inn came into view, I would not awake to find that it had all been a dream, and the sight of those familiar surroundings would stab home the enormity of our loss.

As I watched Andy drive the coach back home over the last few miles, I remembered how shocked he had been when in the early stages of the coach's assembly, someone had inadvertently asked where Herc's door would be. "Why he'll use the same door as Maggie and I", he answered sharply, "He'll use the front door, it's only an animal that uses a separate door". It summed up Andy's views on Herc exactly.

As the Inn came into view I felt nothing. Not for a moment did I feel the usual pleasure at coming home to the place I loved. I didn't want to speak to anyone and dreaded the moment when I would have to answer a question from a customer or member of staff.

Margaret, who helped me with my horses, was the first to meet us, and clearly felt awkward, not knowing what to say. Seeing that we did not want to talk, she kept her greeting brief and we gladly made our way to the privacy of our own flat.

The empty rooms were lonely and silent. the walls covered with photographs and pictures of Hercules recalled the happy times before we left. Idle chatter from the bar drifted up through the floor, and I sat lost in my thoughts waiting aimlessly for the barman to come up and say "that's it for the night", and then I could go and lose myself in sleep.

I realised from the first moment on the first day back that Andy could not accept what fate had dealt him. Always grimly determined, especially when the odds were stacked against him, he refused to give up. "He's still alive, Maggie", he murmured to me in bed that first morning, "somewhere out there in all the wind and rain he is waiting, wondering where his Dad is. I've got to go back, I've got to be there, just in case."

It's strange how a single night can make all the difference, and a new day bring fresh hope to lean upon. "What can I say?" I thought. "How can I, knowing that his heart is breaking, dash even the slightest hope, even if I know that there is none?"

I could see no happy ending, but what could be worse than the ending we already had? And so we prepared for Andy to go back, if only just to be near the scene.

Andy was smiling again as we loaded up his pick-up truck with provisions for him and some of Hercules' favourite food. Always the optimist, Andy believed then, as he believes now, that dreams come true if you believe in them strongly enough.

But I could no longer share his simple faith and, as each day passed with no sign of Hercules, I could only marvel at how when Andy rang to say all his efforts had been useless, he managed to keep any hope alive, for he would end the conversation by saying "perhaps tomorrow, Maggie?"

I felt completely useless sitting at home waiting for news. I could not even ride to take my mind off worrying as I was hardly able to walk because of a twist at the base of my spine. The days seemed utterly bleak, and, as the osteopath worked hard trying to get my back into shape, I tried to plan for the future. Our whole lives were built around Hercules, and I feared the strain it would put on us having to adapt to life without him.

On the eighth day after we had come home I was woken by the telephone ringing. I glanced at my watch and saw it was 7.45 a.m., and just as I was about to get up to answer it, I realised that that my brother Alastair, who had been looking after the Inn in our absence and who had stayed on to keep me company, had already picked up the phone. I heard the click of the receiver as it was quickly replaced.

Rain was lashing against my bedroom window and, having no good reason to get up, I turned over and went back to sleep, but ten minutes later the telephone rang again. Two calls this early in the morning must mean something, but what? I was too scared to even hazard a guess and despite my bad back I leapt out of bed and rushed to the telephone in the next room.

I felt my adrenalin surging as I picked up the phone and listened to the voice at the other end of the line. It was Radio Scotland ringing to ask "is it true that Hercules has been spotted?" he said. "I don't know," I spluttered, not daring to hope. "No one has told me anything."

"Well, Maggie, our news is that he's been spotted and is being tailed by the police who are waiting for Andy to arrive."

"I can't believe it, let me try and find out, I'll ring and get in touch with Andy. Ring me back in 10 minutes."

Shaking, I replaced the receiver and took a deep breath. Alastair came into the room and told me that it was the police from Lochmaddy who had been on the phone earlier. They had asked if Andy was here and had then hung up.

My hands were sweating as I dialled the number for the police station in Lochmaddy. It was answered by Sgt. Anderson's wife, who said "it's true, Maggie", she exclaimed. "They are all out after him now, after he was spotted this morning. A crofter phoned in to say that he had heard a strange crying sound outside his window and when he looked outside it was Hercules. But the cattle in the field had heard him, too, and when they came to have a look, he took fright and they chased him away, poor beastie". She went on "Andy didn't want to build your hopes up again until he was quite sure for himself, so he's out there at the moment."

"My God", I thought out loud "Can I believe it?" I was quivering like a jelly, as I told Alastair the news. I wanted to scream with joy. I grew hot and cold, and the phone started ringing again. It seemed that the media had all heard the news and they sounded just as excited as I was. They had all been involved in their own way, in our disaster and seemed to have a special place in their hearts for Hercules. They all offered me a seat on their various planes, and needless to say, I accepted the first offer.

I stumbled about in my haste to get dressed. As I flung some old clothes into a bag my mind screamed "calm down, calm down, it's probably a false alarm." I grabbed Alastair, who hobbled to the car as fast as he could on a broken leg, and we sped towards Glasgow. I think a broken leg was the least of poor Alastair's problems as he turned paler by the mile, grimly hanging on, with eyes staring ahead, as I tore through the outskirts of Glasgow in my desperate bid to catch the plane.

When we arrive at the airport I jumped out of the car and Alastair took over the controls with a relieved sigh. "Good luck Maggie" he said as he drove off sedately. The weather was getting steadily worse and the cloud level was very low, but the pilot decided that he could make it and soon we were airborne.

As we approached the runway on Benbecula and taxied in to the control tower we could see that the tiny airfield was already crowded with small planes, such as our own, which had brought scores of press-men, reporters and photographers to the scene of the final chase. It all looked like a scene from a Humphrey Bogart film, as the terminal filled with the familiar faces of the press men. All were eager for a good story or the best picture. Yet all these supposedly hard skinned 'seen it all be-fore' reporters wanted a happy ending to their story.

All the taxis the island could supply were mustered and, incredibly, the chase was on again. Archie, our special taxi driver, greeted me with tears in his eyes, his genuine delight at the reappear-ance of Hercules shining through his ruddy face, as we set off to find Andy.

We went round the island, up one road and down the other, re-porters crammed six to a car or more, only to find the ever cheerful Sgt. Anderson and his men soaked to the skin, scrambling down a hill through the heather.

"We spotted him alright Maggie," he said "but some idiot fright-ened him off with their car. He's taken to the hills, up in all that mist", making a sweeping movement over the skyline with his arm. "We've lost Andy too, but he's hardy, he'll be okay" he finished reassuringly. The press all pounced on the sergeant and his men, who though ex-hausted, posed good naturedly for the photographers.

It was five o'clock before we finally caught up with Andy at the white Post Office and store, and after I had almost crushed him to death with my hugs and kisses, he confirmed what Sgt. Anderson had already told us but added ruefully "but he's scared. Completely on the defensive. I think we're going to have to tranquilise him, or he's going to get hurt".

Darkness was closing in earlier than usual because of all the mist and rain, and there was nothing much more that we could do other than to organise ourselves for the next morning. But all the time at the back of our minds was the thought that it had seemed just as straight-forward on the first day that he had disappeared. Even then with the soldiers, dogs, the helicopter and planes we had not been able to find him. We prayed that night that fate would be kinder to us this time.

God moves in a mysterious way and I will always believe that He had a hand in bringing Hercules back to us. At my aunt's house that night as we sat round the peat fire, we received a telephone call from a complete stranger called Allan Mann. He happened to be the owner of a company called Allan Mann Helicopters Ltd., and he was up in the north of Scotland when he had heard of the day's events on the radio. He thought that he might be the answer to our problems and, like an answer to our prayer, he offered us the use of one of his helicopters together with the services of one of his pilots, Captain Akroyd-Hunt, who had nine year's experience in Africa tracing and capturing game. It seemed too good to be true.

Next morning the helicopter made its noisy arrival at exactly 11.00 a.m. On board was our old friend Eddie Orbell and George Rafferty, the vet from the wildlife park. It all seemed miraculous, just like the script of a implausable Hollywood film.

Allan and his pilot quickly refuelled the helicopter and were soon airborne again, with Eddie and George still on board. Soon the helicopter was joined by a fleet of small press planes as they set off in pursuit of Hercules.

Everyone's hopes were high, as they scoured the ground for the first sight of Hercules. But as the day wore on there was still no sight of him. It was hard to believe, but it seemed as though it was all going wrong again.

Andy waited at the pier at Lochmaddy with my father and the coach. My father had rather hurriedly dashed up from the Inn and had crossed over on the ferry to North Uist, Caledonian MacBrayne kindly delaying the ferry so that they could get across. My mother waited at her old home with my bemused grandfather, who couldn't understand what all the fuss was about.

It would soon be time to call a halt to the day's search, and the helicopter would have to fly back to the mainland, and we would be left to face the awful task of searching for Hercules on our own again.

I was flying with Bob Ford-Sagers again, and, like the others, we had not seen a single trace of Hercules all day. As we taxied into the airfield to refuel, we saw that most of the other planes were there for the same reason and some had simply given up. We had been in the air for more than four hours and my eyes were strained from hours of endless searching. I could see only a blur as we made our way to the control tower to join the other despondent crews who were talking in groups, swapping theories, about the puzzling days search.

Suddenly the controller called for silence, and as we eagerly turned towards him we could see him holding one hand up in the air as he pressed the earphones closer to his head. Then we heard the news we had all been waiting for — a crackling transmission from the helicopter crew saying "We've spotted him".

I felt as though my heart would burst. It was beating so hard as more details began to filter through "He's running scared", said the pilot "But we've got to get him now, . . . we're going to use the tranquiliser gun or we'll lose him". A tremendous cheer went up in the crowded smoke-filled room and everyone started to scramble outside. Pressmen fell over each other as they rushed to planes and cars, and there were frantic shouts for telephones. Bob and I decided that we should try to get to the scene, just in case I could be any help.

We got into the car and headed recklessly towards the north of the island, all the constraints of the last few hours suddenly unleashed.

To our dismay we discovered that the helicopter was hovering over a boggy moorland and that there were no through roads. It was yet another frustrating twist, so unable to do anything to help, we headed back to the coach at Lochmaddy.

As we drove back I watched anxiously as the bright orange helicopter lifted and appeared on the skyline with a dark shape hanging below it. My imagination conjoured up a thousand things that might still go wrong. "What if the rope snaps or the net breaks?" I thought as the helicopter swept across the sky, pursued by the ravening hoards of pressmen, camera lenses glittering as they captured the dramatic event on film.

The helicopter was hovering over the playground in Lochmaddy, just as Bob and I came into the town. From a distance I saw Andy's arms outstretched towards the pathetic bundle. He loosened the net, and Hercules was gently lowered into the back of the pick-up truck. My father was at the wheel and he speedily drove Andy and the unconcious Hercules to the coach where he was quickly transferred to the safety of his den.

It seemed as if every inhabitant of the island was there, and they surged around the coach to catch a glimpse of the bear that had captured their hearts over the last few weeks. I struggled through the crowds and was at last reunited with the son that I had given up for lost. Andy was bent over him, kissing his big black nose, crying

H

Running scared

2 tranquilisers and a lassoo, and still going strong . . .

. . . dragging Eddie and George behind him . . .

. . . but at last overcome and secured in the net.

Airborne

Back in Dad's arms

Gently lowered into the pick-up

A very drugged bear

Andy fights back his tears . . .

. . . horrified at the sight of the starved bear . . .

unashamedly. He was not alone, for everyone present seemed to be crying, and only George Rafferty appeared to be calm amidst the chaos as he administered the antidote to the powerful tranquiliser that had been used to subdue the terrified Hercules.

A few minutes after the shot had been put into his much diminished rump, Hercules opened a bleary eye and gave his Dad a great big sloppy kiss. With that he dropped off into a deep sleep.

With tear strained faces Andy and I tried to thank the men responsible for Hercules' safe return, and found ourselves hopelessly inadequate in expressing our gratitude. Eddie explained that one of the helicopter crew had spotted Hercules' ear jutting out from behind a large rock and, as they approached to take a closer look, sheer terror had made him bolt. After running at great speed he had dived into the middle of a peaty loch, and had stayed in the middle completely out of sight apart from his head bobbing on the surface. The helicopter then had to swoop down low over the surface of the water whipping up waves, as they tried to herd him onto the surrounding moorland.

Once driven out of the small loch Hercules started to run again and Eddie fired a shot with the tranquiliser gun, but missed because the draught from the rotor blades blew it off course. His second shot, however, went straight into Hercules' rump. Under the unabating pressure Hercules decided to try and hide again and so made promptly for a deep crevice. There he lay quite still, huddled among the heather.

The helicopter landed and kept its engines running. Eddie and George leapt out, uncertain whether Hercules was by now unconscious or whether he was still conscious and sufficently terrified to turn on them. They managed to put a rope around his neck, but, as they did so and Hercules felt the rope tighten, he was up and running again, driven on by fear alone. He dragged his two captors behind him as he charged up the face of a steep hill, but, as the drug at last began to take effect, he ground to a halt and collapsed. He was quickly rolled into the strong net which was attached to a cable from the helicopter, and unceremoniously lifted into the air and back to Lochmaddy and safety.

We thanked the helicopter crew from the bottom of our hearts, for without them it was doubtful whether Hercules would have survived. The drama was now over and the crew returned to the mainland, the heroes of the day.

Hercules had been missing for 24 days and the effects on him were massive. He had suffered a dramatic, almost fatal loss of weight, having

Safe at long last

lost at least 20 stone since he had disappeared. He now looked like an empty and rather moth-eaten fur coat as he lay huddled at the back of the coach, and we placed a large pillow beneath his head to make him as comfortable as possible.

It was obvious that Hercules had eaten nothing. Far from ravaging the countryside, the poor frightened softy had not even killed so much as a rabbit in order to satisfy what must have been an agonising hunger.

That evening his sleep was so deep that he did not even flinch as I administered the second shot of antidote, and we began to worry that he might be so far gone with exhaustion and hunger that he could not pull through. He should by now have been well awake and neither of us slept as we wondered whether his health would stand the strain.

Next morning Hercules still had not woken, and we could see the bloodsucking ticks that covered his mangy fur. We attacked them with tweezers and disinfectant and as we removed them they left Hercules' skin covered in ugly sores. Meanwhile Hercules was oblivious to the world.

A constant stream of wellwishers came to the coach bringing with them parcels of Hercules' favourite foods — beans, yoghurt, grapes — and when he eventually woke up later that morning, we tried to tempt him with them.

Poor Hercules could not eat a thing. Even the eggs and prawns that he loved so much failed to interest him. He seemed to be unable to chew and anything put into his mouth would pathetically spill out again.

We finally left him to sleep some more, and, worrying what we could do next, we left the coach and walked to my grandfather's house, some 20 yards away. He was still bemused by all the bustling activity that was going on around him and sat puffing his pipe, waiting patiently for my Aunt Effie to produce tea and scones for him.

"Haf you tried him with milk yet, Margaret?" Aunt Effie asked me in her strong Highland accent. "He doesn't like milk much, Effie", Andy replied, shaking his head, while the rest of the household looked on with interest at this new suggestion. "He'll only ever take milk in his tea and coffee". "Oh now I think you should be trying him with some just in case", persisted Effie in her best school-teacher's voice, as she turned to say to her husband's brother "Archie-John, away and get the cow milked to see if poor Hercules will take some fresh warm milk." Archie-John dutifully rose from the table, painfully shy in front of such a crowd and carried the white enamel bucket with him to the byre opposite the house, shouting for the cow as he went. The cow ambled slowly after him and minutes later Archie-John, head bowed, re-appeared carrying the bucket now full of steaming fresh milk.

We all got up and made our way single file out of the back door and walked to the coach, the smell of peat lingered in our nostrils as we tried Hercules with the still warm milk. Success! Like a small calf, he slowly started to suck at the milk in the bottom of the bucket and as he seemed to know that it was doing him some good he greedily slurped at it until every drop was gone. Once again his inbuilt commonsense was helping him to survive.

At last we could begin to completely relax in the knowledge that when Hercules was well, all was well. He was still very weak, but his thirst for milk could not be contained or supplied and so the call went out "The Big Softy needs milk." Supplies started to arrive from all sources, in jugs, buckets, basins and bottles. He drank 40 pints in two days, and all but drank the island dry.

By now, he was able to sit up and watch as visitors came from all over the islands, old and young, and he even managed to entice from her cottage an old woman who had not left her home for almost 20 years.

Amidst all the well wishers arrived a very sorry-looking Sgt. Anderson who whispered to Andy "Could I have a wee word in private with you?" Andy, of course, agreed and we both made our way to the house where Sgt. Anderson told us of his dilemma. "I've had orders from headquarters in Inverness, this isn't from me mind", he said. "But you've to get off the island on the first available boat, and we've to charge you for being here with Hercules". He heaved a sigh and continued, "It's a piece of nonsense, a bloody disgrace if you ask me but I'm sorry Andy, orders are orders." "Well Sgt." said Andy, "You go ahead and charge us, but there's no way we are going until we have been round the schools to let the kids see Hercules".

"But Andy," said the exasperated Sgt. Anderson "I've to charge you for every day you stay on the islands·" He then proceeded to pull out his little black book and told us our rights. Poor Sgt. Anderson, he had worked so hard to get Hercules safely back to us now he was having to carry out some orders from an uninvolved police department on the mainland. We almost thought he would turn mutinous! Sgt. Anderson completed his business and left, still a good friend despite the charges.

No sooner had the word got out than the loyal islanders began to rally around us to give us their full support. Naturally the press picked up the news and began to run articles about the absurdity of the charges, and Caledonian MacBrayne, the ferry company, made Hercules an honorary member, saying that he could travel on their ferries whenever he liked and for free. The ferry employees even said that if Hercules was not allowed to stay on the island for as long he wanted, that nobody would be allowed on or off!

Soon the campaign began to snowball and Andy obtained the services of Joe Beltrami, Scotland's Perry Mason, to defend Hercules. Joe immediately took up the question of the charges against us with the Procurator Fiscal. We were charged with having a dangerous animal on the island and allowing it to escape.

As far as the first charge was concerned, we had a Performing Animals Licence, which meant that we did not need a licence for a dangerous animal, and we thought the second charge was equally unfair, as we had not intended to lose Hercules and it was obvious we had done everything in our power to find him!

The Procurator Fiscal was clearly not happy with the charges, and, so Joe said, he would be prepared to let us off if we applied for a Dangerous Animals Licence. Andy wanted to contest the charges in court but was eventually persuaded by Joe Beltrami that it would not be a good idea to have any blemish on Hercules' record, so we agreed to obtain an additional (and unnecessary) licence and the charges were dropped.

Before we left the island we made a tour of the schools, driving slowly so that Hercules had a smooth ride. Some of the schools had less than 10 pupils, and when they saw Hercules, the smiles that covered their faces seemed to make all our ordeals worthwhile.

It was with great sadness that we left the islands, having found there nothing but a fondness and generosity that we will always remember, but we wanted to get home to complete Hercules' recovery.

California here we come...

9 CALIFORNIA
HERE WE COME

It took several months for Hercules to regain his lost weight and recover physically from his ordeal — mentally his hurts were expressed in a touching reluctance to leave our company.

I fed him as one would an invalid during the weeks following our return home. Foods that were easily digested — steamed fish and mince, milk, yoghurt and plenty of eggs. He spent a lot of time in our sitting room, resting in front of the fire and watching television, and he liked to have Andy or I with him as much as possible. His spirits were high, though, and it didn't look as if any permanent damage of a serious kind had been done.

He was, and still is, frightened of open spaces — it's alright so long as we are about to give him confidence and make him feel secure, but he will not even go into the paddock on his own now. He is clearly scared that what happened to him might happen again.

Another change in him that would be amusing if it wasn't so tragic, and such a vivid reminder of what he must have gone through, is his absolute refusal to jump into deep water. Before, he liked nothing better than to dive into a swimming pool or a loch — now he furtively finds the shallow end of the pool and tests the water for depth with his paw. Unless he can feel or see the bottom he will not go in. This summer Andy and Herc were playing around a swimming pool, chasing each other and romping. Andy would dive in, and poor Hercules so much wanted to join him. He teetered on the edge, time after time, but then always ran down to the steps at the shallow end before entering the pool. We haven't tried him in salt water since his time in the wild, and I'm afraid that he might not take too happily to it, but swimming is still his favourite sport.

These days he prefers to have people about him as many people as possible — and enjoys himself best indoors. He especially enjoys being in crowded places like theatres, where he gains security from the numbers.

Feeling better already

Convalescence can be fun . . .

This is a good thing. After his return from the edge of the world he was a very famous bear indeed. There can have been few people in the whole country who had not heard of him. We were swamped with letters of support and interest, presents and cards, and thousands of visitors. Among the mail came numerous invitations to perform, both in studios and in public theatres and including invitations for several T.V. shows. Had Hercules not been happy about being indoors we would have been unable to introduce him to his admiring public.

One of the major assignments we were offered that winter was to take part in a big variety show in the Playhouse Theatre in Edinburgh with Lena Zavaroni. It would be the most sustained test of Herc's talents so far, as we were billed to perform twice a day for three weeks!

Everybody concerned was very aware that Hercules might not be interested. Quite apart from his ordeal only being three months before, we had to take him up six flights of stairs to reach the stage. Our contract had been carefully worded to take account of the fact that Herc could not be coerced into doing anything he did not want to do. If he didn't like a project then he was intelligent enough to work out a way of putting a spanner in the works, as he had done when we muzzled him, against his will and expected him to wrestle.

We were hopeful, however: if we hadn't been we would never have taken on the job. Hercules' faith in us was so complete by now that we felt sure he would trust us, and once he became used to the unfamiliar situation we were sure that he would enjoy it. Nevertheless, to expect an animal to come up trumps so often, for so long, might be to expect the impossible. If it came off it would be a sensational achievement.

And come off it did, well beyond our expectation. Understanda-

'Don't expect me to jump in . . .'

Birthday celebrations

124

bly, Hercules was a bit nervous to begin with: never before had there been so many people around him and although we knew he was fond of music — especially loud music — which he would listen to from his den as it wafted out of the kitchen, never before had he worked with an orchestra.

From the start, however, everything went perfectly. He romped up the worrying six flights of stairs. He quickly stole the hearts of all the people involved in the production. And, after being initially intrigued by the orchestra and the music, he soon devoted his attention to the audience. Needless to say the audience loved him.

The orchestra was on the stage behind Andy and Hercules, separated from them by a gauze curtain so that the sound they made was not hindered and yet they could be invisible if the scene required it.

Its members became quite used to sharing the stage with an almost full grown grizzly bear and had the security of the gauze curtain between him and them, for what it was worth. Hercules became a great favourite with them. Then on the last day of the show's run, he gave an incredible demonstration of his feelings towards them which was also an uncanny indication of how aware he is of all that goes on around him, and of how talented he is at upstaging everybody else.

By the third week everyone was well into the routine of the production, and although Hercules varied his performance daily and was never predictable, he had grown completely accustomed to what was expected of him. Perhaps it was the sense of excitement that always accompanies the end of a successful show for those taking part in it, perhaps it was pure bravado on Hercules' part.

Whatever it was, suddenly towards the end of the act, he reared up on his back legs, raised his arms above his head and made a bee-line for the gauze curtain separating him from the orchestra. Over eight feet of grizzly bear is enough to fill even the stoutest heart with terror, even when the stout hearts concerned have been working alongside the bear for the previous three weeks. The music ended with many odd squeaks and groans. The orchestra panicked and many tried to escape. Music stands were overturned and chaos ensued. And then the cause of all the fuss calmly stepped back again and swaggered over to his partner.

When it became apparent that the whole thing was 'part of the act' the audience was convulsed, and once they had recovered their composure, so were the members of the orchestra.

It was clear that Hercules knew exactly what he was doing: he had had the last laugh, again, and brought the house down!

Along with the greetings and invitations came honours and awards. The Daily Mirror made him 'Fatty of the month' and their personality of the year. He became Scotland's personality of the year, as well, and the Scottish Tourist Board made him a special award, 'To the Bear with Flair' for bringing so much publicity to the Western Isles. Heineken Beer gave him their Christmas award as the most 'Refreshing Personality of the year', and he was made an honorary member of countless clubs and societies, including one called The Teddy-bears of the World Club. He won a 'humanitarian award' from Animals in America for 'failing to harm any wildlife whilst starving'! The Cartoonist Club of Great Britain gave him their supreme accolade, The Gold Joker of the Year, for the amount of humourous drawings that he had inspired, such as the one in which he was shown sharing a pint with the locals at the pub in Cregorry.

'Me and my lawyer'   Champagne from a silver cup . . .

At the time that he collected this particular award, in the Cartoonists Club, off Fleet Street we were being hounded by an officious man from the Council who believed he had a personal mission to prevent Hercules being seen in public in London. He had been following us around all day, trying to frighten people that we were visiting by telling them that they would be charged if they allowed Hercules into their premises or onto their shows. He arrived at the Cartoonist Club with a band of policemen, and leaving them outside, dashed in to use the telephone. For what reason we didn't stop to find out, for as soon as he was spotted he was surrounded by a mob of our friends in the press who succeeded in keeping him trapped in the call-box until the award had been given and received. He emerged furious and shortly afterwards we were cautioned by the police and later summoned to Bow Street Magistrates Court for not having a Dangerous Animals Licence.

We contacted Hercules' lawyer, Joe Beltrami, and he took the

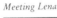

. . . and shandy with beauty-queens

Meeting Lena

advice of senior counsel who said it was quite clear that we didn't need a licence as we already had a performing animals licence. However, Mr Beltrami advised us that, since there was no law against having both licences we should go ahead and get one, which would not only satisfy the English Court but would persuade the procurator fiscal in Inverness to drop his case.

So now Hercules has all the possible licences a bear could need, and he still has an unblemished record with the police. We have decided to introduce him to the United States and Canada and have secured visas to travel there in the New Year. As you can imagine, it is very important to us that we all travel together, Herc in his luxury coach, rather than bundling him into a packing case, as is usually done. This is causing great difficulties.

Originally we thought we would take him in a Hercules jet, which would not only be appropriate, but which is in fact the only air transporter likely to be able to carry him in his travelling den: sadly, this turns out not to be quite big enough, so we will possibly go by sea. Whatever happens, the next chapter of this strange saga will open in the New World, in the land of Herc's fore-bears, and I will tell you all about it in due course.

Who would have thought, only five years ago, that I would have a tale like this to tell? All the experts said it couldn't be done and once it was done our son was lost and all the experts said that he would never be found.

Through hard work, faith and love, rather than facts and theories, the impossible has been achieved and history has been made. Andy and I have been rewarded a thousandfold for our time and effort by the love and trust that we receive in return from this great wild creature. There is a lesson here for all of us.

Maggie Robin

Sheriffmuir, November 1981.